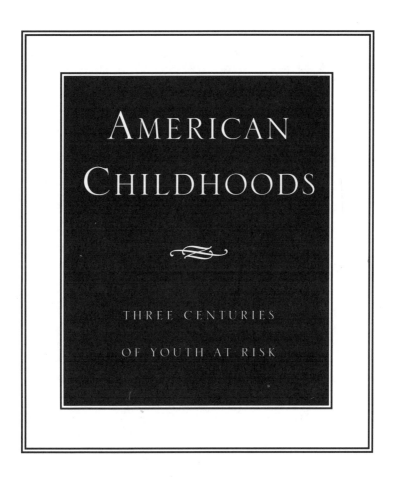

AMERICAN CHILDHOODS

THREE CENTURIES

OF YOUTH AT RISK

RICHARD WORMSER

WALKER AND COMPANY

NEW YORK

To Irma and Earl with many thanks

Copyright © 1996 by Richard Wormser

First published in the United States of America in 1996 by Walker Publishing Company, Inc.

Published simultaneously in Canada by Thomas Allen & Son Canada, Limited, Markham, Ontario

Library of Congress Cataloging-in-Publication Data
Wormser, Richard, 1933–
American childhoods: three centuries of youth at risk/Richard Wormser.
p.   cm.
Includes bibliographical references (p.   ) and index.
Summary: Describes the many hardships America's children have had to endure from colonial times to the present.
ISBN 0-8027-8426-7 (hardcover).
—ISBN 0-8027-8427-5 (reinforced)
1. Children—United States—History—Juvenile literature. 2. Socially handicapped children—United States—History—Juvenile literature. 3. Poor children—United States—History—Juvenile literature. [1. Children—United States—History. 2. Socially handicapped. 3. Poor. 4. Children—Employment. 5. Child abuse.] I. Title.
HQ 792.U5W67 1996
305.23'0973—dc20   96-4152
CIP
AC

The photographs on pages 30 and 33 are used by permission of the Massachusetts Commandery Military Order of the Loyal Legion and the U.S. Army Military History Institute. The photograph on page 70 is used by permission of Moorland-Springarn Research Center, Howard University. The photographs on pages 26, 49, 68, 104, and 121 are courtesy of Covenant House. The photographs on page 40 are courtesy of the Department of Defense. The photographs on pages 15 and 83 are by the author. All other photographs appear courtesy of the Library of Congress.

Book design by Jennifer Ann Daddio
Frontispiece courtesy of Rose Lennon Daddio

Printed in the United States of America

2   4   6   8   10   9   7   5   3   1

Contents

AMERICAN
CHILDHOODS

INTRODUCTION

Adults often complain about how bad the present is—especially when compared with the "good old days." To prove how bad things are today, they point to the rising statistics in crime, the AIDS epidemic, wars that are raging throughout the world, the rise of single-parent families, the failure of many schools to teach children, and the degree of sexual intimacy that exists among teenagers. "Things were much better when I was a child," parents and grandparents insist. But were they? Was the past better than the present? It depends on whose past we're talking about and whose present. Things may have been better for those who grew up in comfortable, middle-class homes where families enjoyed economic prosperity and family values were strong. But were they better for a Puritan child dying from a simple case of measles; an African-American teenager growing up in slavery or segregation; an immigrant child living in a city ghetto; a southern child working in a factory twelve hours a day, six days a week; or a Native-American child whose family was driven off their land by whites?

The past was certainly not a "good old time" for these and millions of other children who had to deal with problems and dangers that few young people today ever experience. It is true that some things were better in the past—family life was generally more stable, drugs were not a widespread problem (although alcohol certainly was), schools were not overwhelmed with discipline problems, and life generally was simpler. But if the "good old timers" could be transported back to the past in a time machine, they would see that many things were worse than they are now. Crime was rampant in the cities, perhaps even more so than today. Children died from disease in appalling numbers. Poor children were brutally exploited in factories. And ethnic and racial prejudice and discrimination were much more prevalent and tolerated.

The young people whose lives are examined in this book were chosen because they represent a cross section of American children from Puritan days to the present. I selected examples of children from different racial, ethnic, and economic groups: black, white, Latino, and Asian; rich, poor, and middle-class. The book draws on many first-person narratives of children selected from either their autobiographies, which they wrote as adults, or letters, diaries, and interviews dating from their youth. Specific individuals were selected because of the richness of their personal experiences as well as their being highly representative of their group.

If most of the lives of the children in this book were unduly harsh, it should be kept in mind that many of them overcame the hardships and made productive and often rewarding lives for themselves as adults. America was a hard place for many young people to survive in the past. Yet, many children of the poor overcame their difficulties and achieved success as adults. They were motivated, in part, by the belief that the United States was a land of opportunity. Today, many disadvantaged young people no longer have faith in the American dream. They see no future and no place for themselves in this society. To bring them into the mainstream of American life is perhaps the most pressing problem that confronts us today.

CRIME AND PUNISHMENT

In August of 1722, a seventeen-year-old teenager climbed a flight of stairs leading to the gallows. Once on the platform, he addressed the crowd that had come to see him hanged.

> I, William Batten, do think it necessary to leave a few lines behind me, that the world may in some measure know something of my past life and what ill use I have made of the time that God was pleased to bestow upon me in this world. . . . without due regard to that which is good, I gave myself up to serve the Devil and to obey his voice by yielding to his Temptations which were lying and picking and stealing other Men's goods.

Batten then began to spell out in detail his crimes of robbery, arson, and murder. When he finished, a hangman placed a rope around his neck, and as a minister prayed for God to have mercy on his soul, William Batten's young life was ended.

In the past, punishment for youthful crimes was far more swift and severe than it is today. The first recorded juvenile execution took place in 1642. While children under fourteen were supposed to be too young to be executed, exceptions were made if it could be proved that they knew "right from wrong." Those children under fourteen who

One of the ways in which Puritans punished people was to put them in the stock-ades. In some cases, children would throw eggs and rotten fruit at them.

were sentenced to death were all nonwhite. Twelve-year-old Hannah Ocuisi was hung in December of 1786 for murdering a six-year-old girl who was about to tell her parents that Hannah had taken some strawberries from her. At the trial, it was shown that Hannah was mentally retarded and had been brutalized as a child. Nevertheless, the judge decreed "she be carried to the place of execution and there be hanged with a rope by the neck, between the heavens and earth until you are dead, dead, dead." The Reverend Henry Channing of Yale college, saddened by Hannah's execution, called her death "a tremendous sentence which puts a period to the life of one who had never learned to live."

Despite harsh colonial laws, juvenile crime was a problem. One group of young people who were often in trouble were poor children from England who had been forcibly taken off the streets of London and sent to America because they were both parentless and often delinquent. Once they arrived, they were forced to work as servants, as were poor American children like William Batten. Many servant children ran away and drifted into a life of crime.

As the problem of juvenile crime increased, the question became how to punish young criminals. In the early days of America, there were few prisons or jails. Offenders over the age of sixteen were often publicly whipped. Some offenders were sentenced to involuntary labor. By the end of the eighteenth century, prisons had been introduced, and six- to twenty-year-olds were sent to the same penitentiaries as adults. Instead of reforming them, prisons educated children about crime. One reformer cried out in protest:

[Children] were cast into a common prison with older culprits to mingle in conversation and intercourse with them, acquire their habits, and by their instruction to be made acquainted with the most artful methods of perpetrating crime.

Eddie Guern, who became a professional criminal, wrote in his autobiography, *I Was a Bandit*, of his first serious arrest at the age of fifteen, when he was put in an adult jail. Guern was brutalized by the guards when he tried to escape.

They put a pair of handcuffs on my wrists, put a hook between them, and dragged me up the stairs and dropped me down again until I almost fainted. For something like ten minutes, they kept up with the torture. Up and down I went, screaming blue murder and calling the warden all sorts of names. I was on the verge of unconsciousness when they finally hauled me up, took the handcuffs and flung me into a dungeon with a bowl of water and a lump of bread to keep me alive.

It was thousands of incidents like these that led to a widespread reform movement in the nineteenth century. More and more states established juvenile institutions in which young people were incarcerated with their peers. In Colorado at the turn of the twentieth century,

Seated behind his desk, Judge Ben Lindsey and his staff listen to a young boy explain why he committed a crime. Lindsey was one of the first judges to emphasize rehabilitation of youth rather than imprisonment.

Judge Ben Lindsey started a crusade for a juvenile justice system in his state. When he ran into political opposition, Lindsey called a meeting in his office and invited the governor, politicians who were both for and against his plan, a few ministers, and the press. He also gathered about twenty boys who had served time in adult prisons. As Lindsey later recalled, "The boys told stories of bestiality that were more horrible because they were so innocently, so baldly given. One boy broke down and cried when he told of the vile indecencies that had been committed on him by older criminals." After the meeting, the opposition to his plan faded.

The new juvenile penal institutions were for both boys and girls. Their purpose was to reform children through the disciplines of work, religion, and education within the facility. The inmates, some of whom had done nothing worse than to flee abusive homes, worked eight hours a day making objects like shoes, nails, and chairs. The goods were sold by local merchants, who profited from the young peo-

All of these teenage boys, whose pictures have been set on tombstones, were hanged for murder in New York in the nineteenth century.

ple's labor and often exploited them. After work, the residents attended classes for several hours, where they learned to read, write, and do simple math.

Even as the pressure built for special treatment for juveniles throughout the nineteenth century, juvenile crime increased. Before the Civil War, many immigrant children grew up in unimaginable poverty. In cities like New York, groups of Irish youth attempted to escape poverty and abusive family life by joining violent and vicious gangs, many of which had colorful names: the Dead Rabbits, Bowery Boys, Forty Thieves, Plug Uglies, Shirt Tails. The gangs were as violent as any of those roaming city streets today. They fought each other with knives, pistols, clubs, and paving stones. At times, more than one thousand members of rival gangs would battle each other, sometimes for as long as two days. The police would not interfere. The gangs also rioted periodically, lynching blacks, burning down the houses of the rich, and attacking the police.

After the Civil War, wave after wave of new immigrants seeking a fresh start in life flooded the major cities of the Northeast. They included Italian families escaping the tyranny of landlords in southern Italy and Sicily, Germans escaping political persecution, and Jews from Russia who were driven from their homeland by anti-Semitism. They were joined by African-Americans who were, despite the abolition of slavery, still struggling to secure a foothold in the United States.

Instead of opportunity, the immigrants found hardship, misery, and the worst forms of poverty. The children quickly organized into gangs based on neighborhood and ethnicity. Irish, Italians, Jews, Bohemians, and African-Americans fought each other. These gang wars were not as vicious as previous gang wars, perhaps because family influence seemed to be greater. Guns, although not difficult to obtain, were seldom used. Killings were rare. And sometimes young people from different ethnic groups who lived on the same block would belong to the same gang.

The common enemy that often united the gangs was the police. A constant state of war existed between the gangs and the police. Police officers often took sadistic pleasure in harassing children. In *Jews Without Money* Mike Gold, who grew up in the early twentieth century, remembered:

There was no such character as the kindly cop on the beat. The cops were sworn enemies. By the same token, we street

This gang, called the Dead Rabbits, was one of the worst gangs in nineteenth-century New York and as vicious as any gang today.

kids were the biggest source of trouble for the police. We accounted for most of the petty thievery and destruction of property. And since we couldn't afford to pay off the cops, they hounded us, harassed us, chased us, and every chance they got, happily beat the hell out of us.

Despite their feuds, the gangs warned each other when their common enemy was lurking. Harpo Marx, who became a famous comedian and movie star, recalled:

The only way all of us kids stuck together regardless of nationality was in our cop warning system. Much as I loathed and feared the Mickie gang or the Bohunk gang, I'd never hesitate to give them the high sign if I spotted a copper coming their way. They'd do the same for me.

It was dangerous to be caught on some other gang's territory. The intruder would be caught, beaten, humiliated, and robbed before he was let go. Mike Gold remembered how a strange kid would be interrogated.

The East side for children was a world plunged into eternal war. It was suicide to walk into the next block. Each block was a separate nation and when a strange boy appeared, the patriots swarmed.

"What streeter?" was demanded furiously.

"Chrystie Street," was the trembling reply.

BANG! This was a signal for a mass assault on the unlucky foreigner, with sticks, stones, fists and feet. The beating was cruel and bloody. No mercy was shown. I had three holes in my head and many black eyes from street wars. We did it to the others, they did it to us.

When the gangs weren't fighting each other, they were often stealing. Petty theft was a common practice in the ghetto and often approved by parents who shared in the proceeds, especially if food was involved. Leonard Covello, who came from Italy, worked abandoned buildings. "We stole lead from the primitive plumbing to sell to the junk man. We stole bricks and chipped off mason [sic] and sold them again."

It is not surprising that many young people graduated into more serious crime. But a criminal life held many dangers. There were some who preyed on children to make thieves and beggars out of them. Edward Mulhearn was fourteen when he ran away from home in Jersey City to find work in New York. Instead he met a man named David Smith, who was kind to him at first. According to a report of the Society for the Prevention of Cruelty to Children:

[Smith] drew his attention to the careless way ladies carried their bags and purses and the easy thing it was to get them.

As preparation for joining gangs of older boys, young boys would form their own gangs and fight with other bands of children.

He induced Edward to try his hand. Edward tried and won. He was richer by three dollars! It did seem easy. From that time on Smith took Edward on a number of thieving raids, but he never seemed to become adept enough to be trusted out of range. When he went out alone, he returned empty-handed. This did not suit Smith. It was then he conceived of turning this inferior little thief into a superior beggar. He took the boy into his room and burned his arms with a hot iron. The boy screamed and entreated in vain. The merciless wretch pressed the iron deep into the tender flesh and afterwards applied acid into the raw wounds. . . . Thus prepared, Edward was sent out every day by this fiend who never let him out of his sight and threatened to burn his arm off if he did not beg money enough. He begged hard and handed Smith the pennies faithfully. He received bad food and treatment in return.

These boys showed the cameraman how they robbed a drunk.

As professionals tried to get at the root of juvenile crime, they began to look for causes. The media were blamed by some, just as movies, video games, and music are today. One newspaper editor interviewed Jesse Pomeroy, a fifteen-year-old who had murdered two children. He tried to prove that Pomeroy was motivated by the trashy dime novels that glorified violence, much as comic books do today. Pomeroy wasn't sure whether such books caused his crimes but condemned them anyway.

Editor: What were the books about?

Pomeroy: Killin' and scalpin' injuns and running away with women.

Editor: Were there any pictures in the books?

Pomeroy: Yes sir, plenty of them. Blood and thunder pictures. Tomahawking and scalping.

Editor: Do you think these books inspire you to do what you have done?

Pomeroy: Yes sir. It seems to me that they did. I can't say exactly of course. Perhaps if I should think it over, I should say it was something else.

Editor: Would you advise the other boys not to read this [type of] book?

Pomeroy: Indeed sir, I would.

Throughout the first decades of the twentieth century, young people in trouble were increasingly treated as a special category by almost every state. But race played a large part in the process. White children always received more consideration than blacks. In the 1940s, when George Stiney, a fourteen-year-old black youth, was accused of killing two little white girls in South Carolina, he was found guilty in minutes and executed within months. His lawyer refused to appeal the case. Even white people in South Carolina pleaded for the boy's life, protesting he was too young to die. A sheriff who attended his execution, and supported the death penalty, objected to Stiney's execution on the grounds of his youth. He said that when Stiney was strapped into the electric chair, his wrists were too small to be secured by the straps on the chair. But the state had its way, and he was killed.

After World War II, juvenile crime was once again associated with street gangs. In ethnic neighborhoods, teenagers organized around group loyalties. Gangs fought each other to protect their "turf." The battles were often violent. Chains, baseball bats, metal bars, and knives were used, but seldom guns. While many received serious injuries in these battles, few were killed.

As whites fled the cities for the suburbs in the 1950s, gang warfare among white ethnic groups decreased while the number of Hispanic and black gangs—whose members were trapped in urban ghettos—increased. By the 1970s, two new elements had been introduced into the gang world: drugs and guns. Youth gangs discovered that they could make huge amounts of money in the drug trade—more than they could by working at legitimate jobs. Many children saw selling drugs as their only way out of poverty. To protect their interests, as well as their territories, gangs became increasingly violent. Guns were extremely powerful, easy to buy, and easy to use. Eleven-year-olds celebrated their first kill in a drive-by shooting while funerals for fourteen-year-olds were common. Human life—one's own or someone else's—had little value. Loyalty to the gang and neighborhood was the highest form of loyalty. A member of the Los Angeles Crips, one of the most violent gangs in the nation, described his attitude:

I don't feel connected to any other kids in this city, or in this country or in this world. I only feel comfortable in my hood. That's the only thing I'm connected to. That's my family. One big family.

Gang members were expected to devote their life and energies to *gang banging*—that is, gang activities. The highest values within the gang were respect and reputation. G. Rock, a gang member interviewed by León Bing in her book on Los Angeles gangs, *Do or Die,* explained the importance of reputation:

[All] I'm trying to do is make a name for myself. I'm trying to have a bad rep. Be a straight criminal, be devious, do anything, be bad to the fullest. Anybody want to fight, we can fight. Anybody want to shoot, we can shoot. Anybody want to kill, . . . we can kill.

While some of the violence of gang warfare has diminished recently, often as a result of the work of community organizations, the underlying conditions that breed gangs and gang warfare remain. In poor communities, where job opportunities are relatively few, drug dealing still attracts many. Numerous gang members feel rage against a society that continues to be deeply prejudiced against minorities. Rather than suppress this rage, many youths are now willing to act it out violently. As one Crips gang member put it: "It doesn't matter if anybody understand it or not. We just bringing home the hate. That's the kind of a world we live in."

Gang crimes, however, are only part of the total picture. Juvenile crimes of all sorts dominate today's headlines. A thirteen-year-old boy lures a two-year-old into the woods and strangles him. A sixteen-year-old youth opens up his backpack, removes a nine-millimeter pistol, and pumps eleven bullets in a twelve-year-old who he claimed "dissed" him the day before. A child becomes an expert car thief by the time he is seven, although his feet cannot reach the pedals. A fourteen-year-old girl kills her father for sexually abusing her. Every day, newspapers report about increasing violence in the schools, on the streets, within the homes. Congresspeople and parents, ministers and educators quote the escalating statistics of juvenile crime and warn that violence among young people today is the worst it has ever been in the nation's history.

One consequence of juvenile crimes is that the courts have come down hard on juvenile

Every year, millions of teenagers are arrested, and a growing number are being sent to juvenile jails or prison if their crime is serious enough.

offenders. Children thirteen and older are now tried as adults if the crime is serious enough and involves violence and the threat of violence. Calvin Barnes was fourteen years old when he was convicted of brutally beating a man to death in a robbery. He was sentenced to serve a minimum of thirty years in prison before being eligible for parole. Charles Halleck was sixteen when he was given life (twenty-five years) plus an additional fourteen years for car theft involving a hold-up murder in which he was waiting outside the store when the crime was committed. Gary Graham has been on death row for fifteen years for a crime he was convicted of when he was seventeen. Terry Roach was also seventeen when he was sentenced to death for murder. He was eventually executed at the age of twenty-nine. At least a dozen other juveniles are presently waiting on death row to see if the courts will uphold or overturn their convictions.

Does death for juveniles have a deterrent effect? There is no evidence that it does. As David Bruck, a death-row lawyer, states, "The only purpose that killing teenagers for crimes seems to serve is that it makes the criminal justice system more brutal. If a society cannot do something better than legally execute its children, then something is radically wrong with that society."

DYING YOUNG

When a young person dies from a disease today, it is so unusual that people are shocked. For many people, it is hard to imagine young people dying from illness because medical science has made such progress in discovering cures for so many diseases. Yet until recent times, young people—especially children—were more likely to die from disease than adults.

In Puritan America one out of every two children died before they reached their teens, and the average life span was thirty-two years. It was so common for children to die that a minister once preached a sermon that began, "Children it is your dawning time. It may also be close to your dying time." Cotton Mather, who was a famous New England minister, fathered fifteen children, only two of whom survived him. His wife and three of his children died in one week from the measles.

One reason that so many children died was because people were ignorant about the causes of illness and the need for sanitation. Most colonists did not take baths. They washed their hands and face but little else—unless they happened to swim in a river or lake. There were no toilets, and sewerage was often located near a water supply. Children died from minor ailments like sore throats and common colds, which sometimes developed into pneumonia. They contracted cholera and smallpox, diphtheria and dysentery.

Epidemics of these diseases were common. In 1735, in the parish of Hampton Falls, New Hampshire, 210 people died from diphtheria out of a total population of 1,200! Of those stricken 95 percent were younger than twenty years of age. Twenty families in the community lost all their children. Philadelphia lost several thousand children when an epidemic of yellow fever struck the city in 1794.

Death was a major theme in children's stories. Children's books were filled with stories of children dying with joy because they believed they were on their way to heaven. One of the most popular books of early colonial times had the extraordinarily long title of: *A Token for Children being an Account of the Conversion, Holy and Exemplary Lives and Joyful Deaths of Several Young Children by James Janeway. To which Is Added a Token of New England of Some Examples of Children in Whom the Fear of God Remarkable Budding before They Died in Several Parts of New England; Presented and Published for the Encouragement of Piety in Other Children.*

Medical treatment in those days was primitive, and children received the same treatments as adults. Doctors tried to cure illness by bleeding patients, that is, by removing large quantities of blood from their bodies. They believed that by draining blood, they were physically removing the disease from the body. Medicines were often of little use and contained strange ingredients. Snail water—water in which snails were kept—was a common prescription. A hot onion held to the ear was used to treat earache. For a stomachache, children drank burned brandy and water. The treatment for thrush, an infant disease of the throat, was to hang a live frog tied in a bag around the baby's throat. Parents hung wolf's fangs and deer teeth around their children's necks to protect them from disease. It is no wonder that many children died from the cures rather than the diseases.

By the nineteenth century, medicine had not improved much. For those children who made the grueling journey in covered wagons to settle in the Midwest or on the Pacific coast, death was an ever-present companion. Many children died from accidents on the trip, often stumbling and falling under the wheels of wagons or drowning while

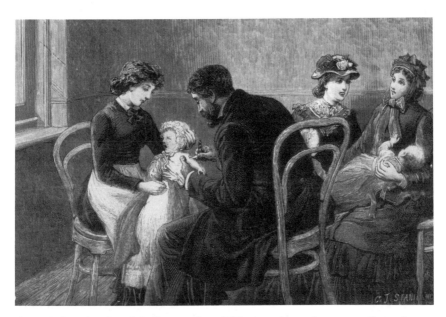

One of the most dreaded diseases that children could catch was smallpox. It was usually fatal, until a vaccine was developed that protected children from the illness.

trying to cross swollen rivers. But the worst killer of children was again disease: mountain fever, pneumonia, and the dreaded cholera. Because people were still ignorant about the causes of cholera, they drank contaminated water and caught the disease in this way. Cholera attacked the intestines and dehydrated them. Unable to eat or drink, they turned and tossed in feverish agony, their lips parched and cracked, racked by diarrhea, until they died or recovered. Mary Todd, who was fifteen, watched her younger sister hover between life and death before she recovered.

> Sometimes father thought she was gone but I heard him repeating the twenty-third Psalm; when he came to "Yea, though I walk through the shadow of the Valley of Death," he seemed to stop so I took up the lines and said, "for thou art with me." . . . She lay so still, stretched out never moving a hand or anything, looking as if she were gone.

Children were more accepting about death in the nineteenth century, perhaps because of their strong belief in a life-after-death. When one girl realized that she was about to die, she instructed her mother to dig a grave six feet deep for she did not want the wolves to "dig her up and eat her." She told her parents to "pile a lot of rocks on her grave after they covered it up right."

Whole families and groups of friends died on the trail. One woman wrote home about the fate of her relatives and friends who had made the western journey.

> Huffmaster and wife and Manerad are dead. Uncle Enos is dead. Craig and wife and child are dead. David's child is dead. Belson's crippled child got shot by moving a gun as she got into the wagon. She lived about an hour. Even Hanen's child died. Stephen's child died. Nancy Graham and William Ingram's children are dead. Jacob Rushe's widow and child are dead. Elvy Hanen is delirious and an object to look at.

Sometimes, parents died but their children survived. Others usually took in the orphans but not always. One traveler recorded:

> I was one day traveling alone when I overtook a little girl who had lingered behind her company. She was crying and as I took her in my arms, I discovered that her little feet were bleeding by coming in contact with the sharp stone upon the road. I said, "why do you cry, does your feet hurt you, see how they bleed." "No (she says) nothing hurts me now. They buried my mother and father now and I don't want to live any longer. They took me away from my sweet mother and put her in the ground."

Pioneer children were not free from danger even when they had safely arrived at their destinations. Even in the most isolated regions, disease found its way into the home. Diphtheria was one of the worst childhood diseases in the nineteenth century. It attacked the throat of its victim and blocked it with a membrane, making breathing increasingly difficult. Children suffered hallucinations as a result of a lack of oxygen to the brain and suffocated to death.

The settlers not only contracted diseases but spread them to those around them. More Native Americans died from the white man's illnesses than were killed in battle. Native Americans had no immunity to these diseases. Whole tribes were wiped out by smallpox, cholera, dysentery, measles, and mumps. Even on the trail, pioneer children passed the half-buried bodies of Indians who died. Mary Todd remembered one such discovery:

> At one place, I noticed John [her brother] peeping into what seemed to be a deserted teepee. My curiosity was aroused and I wanted to see too. So I skipped over there and looked in. To my horror, I saw, partly covered by a buffalo robe, a stack of dead Indians! Their hands and feet were sticking out. Starting to run through the tall grass to our wagon, what should I do but come across another one lying in the grass. I was going at such a speed that I had to jump over this one.

If children were vulnerable to disease in open country where their nearest neighbor might be ten miles away, health conditions were a thousand times worse in the large cities where many people might crowd into a single room. Between 1815 and 1914, over thirty-five million people immigrated to the United States, many of them jammed into overcrowded city ghettos. Poor city children lived in tenement buildings. These buildings were four to five stories high, with no elevators, and as many as six people—or even more—shared a room. The two most striking features of the tenement were the darkness of the halls and the odors. One building inspector compared them to coal mines. "The most barbarous parts of the building are the halls. A person coming in from the sunlight outside plunges into these halls

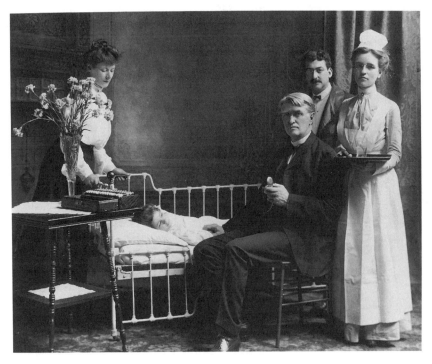

In the nineteenth century, doctors had an imperfect understanding of the causes and treatments of disease. With few exceptions, none of the available medicines were effective against childhood illnesses.

just like a car filled with men plunges and disappears into the black mouth of a mine shaft."

The children of immigrants grew up in the poorest, filthiest, and most diseased part of the city. Sewers were always overflowing, bodies of dead horses lay in the streets for days, starving cats and dogs fought for scraps of food, and rats gorged themselves on the mountains of garbage and rotting food that piled up in backyards and alleys. The apartments were often filthy. Sometimes there was only one toilet for every two floors of apartments, and frequently that was not working. There was no running water. Women had to lug heavy buckets, filled with water at an outside pump, up many flights of stairs. The food was often rotten. Flies were everywhere.

Diseases thrived in such an environment. Children died by the thousands of smallpox, cholera, diphtheria, and pneumonia, or wasted away with the "scourge" of the ghetto: tuberculosis. Some people called it the "plague." One investigator noted that in one filthy apartment in which seven families lived one after another, at least one member of each family caught tuberculosis and died. In another apartment, he found a family where the father had died from tuberculosis, the mother was ill, and the main support of the children was a dying daughter.

> The girl of sixteen lived for three months on tea and bread alone working each day for four dollars a week in a factory pushing a heavy treadle from 6 in the morning to 7 at night. She had worked so since she was 12. "She ain't never seen the country," said her little sister, who loved her. She went to night school always. She said she wanted to be somebody. She took up with the plague in the winter when the coal had gone up and when the sleepless nights were freezing cold. She now knows what the cough means when it shakes her thin, hollow chest; and her eyes have that pitiful haunted look which young eyes must ever have when suddenly meeting death.

But even as the slums were breeding disease and pestilence, a major change in medical treatment was taking place. Scientists had discovered that disease was caused by germs, not, as so many then believed, by unhealthy air or God's will. For the first time, a scientific treatment of illness was possible. Physicians and health-care specialists learned that dirt and poor sanitation were prime causes of disease. A campaign was launched throughout the major U.S. cities, and the public schools, to promote cleanliness and health. One campaign was called "swat a fly." Flies had been identified as carriers of disease, and a campaign was launched in 1916 to kill as many of them as possible.

While most diseases afflicted the poor, whom many of the middle class and rich considered "morally inferior" and therefore more susceptible to disease, there was one dreaded illness that seemed to strike the

This is an advertisement for a painkiller. Many people relied on patent medicines, which were of little use in curing illness. However, since many contained a high percentage of alcohol or often codeine, they worked as temporary painkillers.

children of the well-to-do. It was infantile paralysis, known as polio, and its cure was to remain undiscovered until after the Second World War. Polio was a disease that, in its severe form, could kill or completely paralyze a child. Parents and children were more frightened of it than of any foreign enemy. Franklin Delano Roosevelt, who was president of the United States between 1933 and 1945, caught the disease as an adult and could never walk again.

The fact that polio seemed to favor the wealthier class shocked and irritated some. It seemed that poorer children had stronger immune systems against polio, being surrounded by so much disease. One Philadelphia newspaper reporter wrote, "There was considerable agitation in the exclusive district along the Main Line when the news became current that infantile paralysis had penetrated the exclusive community where immigrants are not allowed."

In response to the disease, parents isolated their children. Since it struck in the summer, they often sent them away to remote places, kept them indoors at home, and limited the number of friends they could have contact with during the dangerous season. They were forbidden to attend any public recreation, like movies and theaters; nor could they go to stores or use public transportation. For thirty years, usually during the summer, each epidemic struck tens of thousands of children. In 1952, one of the worst years, almost sixty thousand children were stricken. But time was on the side of science. By 1956, a vaccine was developed to prevent polio.

Polio was a dreaded childhood disease that crippled hundreds of thousands of children before a vaccination was found to prevent it.

Today, there are no major diseases in the United States that target large numbers of children. Those who do become ill usually suffer from diseases that afflict the general population. Every year some eleven thousand young people under the age of twenty develop cancer, but whereas once they would have died within a year or two, most survive five years or longer. To do so, they live in a world of chemotherapy, amputations, radiation, and isolation.

The most serious disease that plagues young people today is AIDS. It is spread by intravenous drug use and unprotected sex. While the number of high school students diagnosed with AIDS makes up less than 8 percent of the total cases, a relatively low figure, almost 24 percent of the AIDS population is between the ages of twenty to

While it is still rare for young people today to contract serious illnesses, the numbers are rising because of an increase in sexual activity and the use of drugs.

twenty-six. Since the disease takes several years to incubate, most of these young adults were infected in their teens.

Teenagers with AIDS bear a double burden. Not only will they die young, but most have to keep their affliction a secret if they are to have any kind of social life. They do not want to risk confiding in others for fear of rejection. One eighteen-year-old listening to his classmates talk about AIDS was convinced that his decision not to reveal his condition was the right one.

They talked about sending everyone with AIDS to an AIDS Island and turning it [into] something like a Club Med for those of us who are HIV positive. That night I laid awake for

a long time and wondered what would happen if I told them I
was infected.

Another teenager felt that whatever chance he had for a normal life
while in school would be ruined if people knew.

I'd be so embarrassed if everyone knew that I was HIV positive. Now when I go out drinking with the guys, they'll ask for
a sip of what I'm having. They wouldn't do that anymore if
they knew about my disease. They'd treat me differently.

One teenager told her best friend that she was HIV positive.
When the friend passed on this news to her own father, he forbade
her to see the teen again. However, revealing that one is HIV positive
or has AIDS does not always elicit a negative response. One teenager
told his girlfriend, who, despite his fears, did not reject him.

The fact that so many young people die from AIDS is particularly
tragic. Unfortunately, instead of compassion and understanding, victims of the disease often encounter hostility and condemnation from a
fearful public. While a cure for AIDS seems remote at the present
time, so too did cures for polio, diphtheria, and other diseases. If the
past is any guide, we may have reason to hope that one day in the near
future, medical science will also discover a cure for AIDS.

The AIDS epidemic demonstrates that new diseases can erupt at
any time. And while most of the terrible afflictions of the past have
been brought under control with antibiotics and other medications,
these cures themselves can sometimes open the door to new infections.
New variations of old diseases like tuberculosis have developed resistance, if not immunity, to antibiotics. While there is little chance that
young people will be stricken with diseases of the past, the potential
of the diseases of the future—often related to a young person's life-
style—may pose an even greater threat.

WARRIOR CHILDREN

Until World War I, boys fourteen and younger served as soldiers in the American army. Some as young as six were musicians and aides in the army and marines, and deckhands and cartridge carriers in the United States Navy. Many famous generals and politicians served as boy soldiers—including President Andrew Jackson who, at the age of fourteen, was an officer's aide during the American Revolution. Jackson was captured by the British and imprisoned because he refused to accept a menial job. As he later recalled, "A lieutenant tried to make me clean his boots and cut me with a saber when I refused. After that they kept me in jail two months, starved me nearly to death and gave me the smallpox."

When West Point was opened in 1834, boys as young as twelve were admitted. One youth wrote to his mother, "It would astonish you I think to see little boys not four feet high touch off a large cannon and performing all the different duties necessary to a man."

The routine was hard. The boys awoke at dawn, studied math, then cleaned their rooms and weapons. After breakfast, they attended math class from eight to eleven, studying arithmetic, geometry, and trigonometry. From eleven to one, they studied French, the international language of the day. After lunch, the boys continued their French studies until four. From four to sunset they drilled, practicing

Many of the soldiers who fought in the American Revolution were young boys between the ages of fourteen and sixteen.

their drumming and marching. After supper, they studied math until bedtime at half past nine.

In the navy, before there was a naval academy at Annapolis, young boys served as cabin boys on ships—running errands for the ship's officers. Older boys were "powder monkeys," an extremely dangerous job in which they carried ammunition from the powder magazine to guns during battle. A spark could cause an explosion. Those who had enough education to qualify as future officers in the navy were made midshipmen, a sort of junior officer. By the age of twelve, every midshipman was supposed to know the manner of rigging and stowing on ships, how to handle artillery at sea, and how to navigate and make astronomical calculations.

In the days before radio communications, music was employed to communicate military commands to the troops because voice commands could not be heard in battle. Music played by drummers and fifers was used to communicate commands and direct charges, troop movements, and maneuvers. The most famous use of a musical instrument in battle was the bugle used in cavalry charges.

Drummers were used for a number of military ceremonies. Every time a man was physically punished—flogging was common in the

One of the most dangerous jobs in the navy was that of powder monkey. Powder monkeys brought ammunition to the gunners during battle.

army—the drummers played as the blows were struck. Augustus Meyers, a twelve-year-old drummer boy who served in the army in 1854, recalled one such punishment in his memoirs.

> One of the boys was lashed face down on a bench and held by a number of guards at his head and on his feet. His clothes were removed to expose his buttocks and a corporal commenced to apply the rattan [a bamboo stick] which left a red mark at every stroke and made the boy cry out in pain.

Drummers were also called on to play a song called "The Rogues March" for soldiers who deserted and were kicked out of the army. Because the ceremony was accompanied by drum music, the process was called being "drummed" out of the army. The deserters were first marched past the troops with the drummers playing behind them.

They were stripped, their heads were shaved, their hips branded with the letter *D* for "deserter," and they were tied to posts and beaten. Army tradition required drummers to administer the beating. When Meyers's turn to administer this punishment came, he refused. He was court-martialed and sentenced to ten days in solitary confinement, twenty days hard labor, and the loss of one month's pay. But he would not compromise his principles. Once free, he was never again asked to administer a beating.

Boys who were not yet in their teens often served as army drummers. Drums were used to signal commands to troops.

The patriotism of the boys who enlisted was intense. When the Civil War broke out, children as young as seven tried to enlist as musicians. George Ulmer, a Maine boy whose nickname was Cully, was seized with a fierce patriotism to join the army. He was twelve but small for his age and looked younger. When he was finally accepted, it was a great day in his life. Because he was so small, the army had no uniform to fit him. He had to roll his pant legs up to his knees. His overcoat dragged on ground. He commented, "The smallest coat looked like it would make a suit for my whole family."

George Ulmer (Cully) was one of the most famous of the Union Army drummers.

Despite his age, Cully was treated like any other soldier. The only exception was that he was not as closely supervised as regular soldiers and had a great deal of freedom to come and go from the camp. He ate the same food as the others, which was mostly salt pork and hardtack (hard biscuits), bread and beef, and occasionally blackberries and milk. Much of the time, he went out on "foraging" expeditions, which was a polite word for stealing from local farmers. Although the army was supposed to provide enough food for the soldiers, everything was so badly organized—especially when the army was on the march—that they usually did not have enough food to eat or clothes to keep them warm. Cully became an expert chicken thief and once even killed an old cow and cut her up for meat. If a hog happened to stray from its farm, the men would have fresh pork that night. When Cully was caught on occasion, his youth often saved him from punishment.

No matter how well a boy carried out his duties in camp, his ultimate test was how he would do in battle. Cully's first battle was a nightmare.

I found myself amidst bursting shells and heavy musket fire. I was bewildered and frightened. I did not know which way to go. Every turn I made, I seemed to encounter more bullets and shells. Soldiers were running in every direction. Artillery was galloping here and there. On one side of me I saw horses and men fall and pile up on top of one and another, caissons were turned upside down, riderless horses were scampering here and there, officers were riding and running in all directions. The shells were whizzing through the air and soldiers shouting at the top of their voices. Dead and dying heroes were lying thick about. Blue and gray mingled together on this awful field of slaughter. . . . A Union officer shared his water with a Confederate soldier who had lost a leg. A Confederate was stopping the life blood of a Union officer from spilling out by winding his suspenders

African-Americans were supposedly forbidden to serve in the Union forces, yet many young black men did.

around his mangled arm. Everything seemed upside down. I thought that the world had come to an end.

During combat, drummer boys had to be sent into the front line to signal the troops. As shells and musket fire burst around them, they calmly played their musical commands. Although many were scared, few ever broke ranks and ran. Being called a coward was far worse than being killed or wounded. Even though soldiers on both sides generally tried to avoid shooting at drummers and fifers, there were casualties. One officer described the funeral of Clarence, a twelve-

Drum corps like this one marched into battle ahead of the troops. Generally, soldiers tried to avoid firing at them.

year-old drummer boy killed in action, who was a favorite of the troops.

> As the coffin was taken from the drummers' quarters, preceded by the balance of the drum corps, a fifer played the slow and solemn tune of the Dead March, the other companies of the regiment fell into line and followed it. Many a man who would not flinch in battle shed tears over the remains of poor Clarence. He was the smallest in the corps and liked by everyone who knew him.

A number of boys were injured or killed because of their immaturity and impulsive behavior. Cully met a drummer boy on a hillside who was trying to drive a stake into the ground using an unexploded rebel shell as a hammer. Cully warned him of the danger, but the Pennsylvania teenager ignored him. "Rebel shells were duds," he said. Suddenly there was an explosion.

> The poor fellow lay unconscious and covered with blood. There was hardly a shred of clothing on him. His hair was all

burned and both hands had been taken completely off as if done by a surgeon's saw. The sight was horrible but I quickly regained my composure —knowing that something must be done and quickly; so taking the snares from my drum, I wound them tightly around his wrists to stop the flow of blood. The poor fellow regained consciousness and looked at his mutilated wrists. "God Damn! Tough ain't it." Then with tears in his eyes he broke down. "Oh my God. What will my poor mother say! What will my poor mother say! Oh what will she do?"

Drummer boys were known for their courage and were often wounded in battle, especially if they became involved in the fighting.

Some drummer boys won the congressional Medal of Honor for heroism on the battlefield. Nathaniel Guynne was fourteen when he ran away from home to join the army. At the second Battle of Cold Harbor, he was shocked to see that the Confederates had captured his regiment's colors. Every regiment, Northern and Southern, had its own flags, or colors, and it was a source of great pride to the regiment to carry those flags into battle. It was considered a disgrace to lose the colors to the enemy. When Guynne saw his colors in the hands of the enemy, he picked up a musket, clubbed the Confederate soldier holding them, and grabbing his regiment's flags, headed back to his own lines. The Confederates fired at his arm to get him to drop the flags. He was struck so many times that his arm was literally shot away. He shifted the flag to the other arm, and even though he was shot in the

A young Sioux warrior in his traditional dress for battle with his tomahawk, bow and arrows, and shield. Later on, most Native-American warriors had rifles as well.

legs as well, Nathaniel managed to crawl back to his lines. For his courage, he was awarded the Medal of Honor.

Even as the Civil War raged, another war was going on in this country, a war in which other boys and young men were eager to fight. The fight was between Native Americans and the settlers who were trying to take their land away from them. Although there had been occasional battles between tribes before the white settlers arrived, tribal wars gave way to a war against a common enemy.

For almost every Native American boy growing up, battle was the ultimate test of manhood. Boys were prepared to become warriors at an early age. Sioux children played war games, riding naked on horses and fighting each with mud balls and willow sticks. The ponies would clash and scream as the youths tried to throw each other to the ground. It was a great day for a boy when he was allowed to join in a real conflict. Iron Hawk, a Hunkpapa Sioux, fought in his first battle against American soldiers when he was fourteen; it was the Battle of the Little Bighorn, in which General George Armstrong Custer was killed.

I went into the teepee and got dressed for war as fast as I could but I could hear the bullets whizzing around my tent and I

Many young Sioux warriors fought in the famous Battle of the Little Bighorn in which General George Armstrong Custer and his troops were killed.

was so shaky that it took me a long time to braid an eagle feather in my hair. . . . While I was doing this, crowds of warriors on horses were roaring by yelling "Hola Hey." Then I rubbed paint over my face, took my bow and arrows and got on my horse. I did not have a gun, only arrows. . . . Little Bear rode up to me and said, "Take courage boy. The earth is all that lasts." . . . We saw soldiers running downhill towards us. . . . We all yelled "Hola hey" and charged towards them riding all around in the twilight that had fallen on us. I met a soldier on horseback and let him have it. The arrow went through from side to side under his ribs and stuck out at both sides. He screamed and took hold of his saddle horn and hung on, wobbling with his head down. I kept along beside him and I took my heavy bow and shot him across the back of the neck. He fell off the saddle and I beat him to death with my bow. Every time I hit him I said "Houah." I was thinking of the women and little children running down there all scared and

out of breath. The Wasichus [whites] wanted it, and they came
to get it, and we gave it to them.

The end of the wars against the Wasichus meant that Native-
American youth would no longer fight in battles. Nor would American
youth under seventeen be allowed to join the military after World War
I. Drummers and fifers had become obsolete as radio communications
replaced music, and warfare became increasingly technological. While
a few boys as young as sixteen lied about their age and joined the army,
most teenage soldiers were eighteen.

Until the Vietnam War, young men were proud to serve their
country. They believed that they were fighting to save the United
States from an enemy, whether it was Germany and Japan in World
War II or North Korea and China in the Korean War. But in the
1960s, for the first time U.S. soldiers found themselves engaged in a
war that many Americans considered immoral. Many thought that the
war was justified because it was against communism, whereas others
felt that the war was primarily a civil war within a country that had
been arbitrarily divided by the Western powers. The United States,
they believed, had no business interfering.

Not only did the Vietnam War deeply divide the country, it created a tremendous upheaval within the military itself. Many young
men in their teens were the primary victims. They suffered psychological damage from the brutality of the fighting, became addicted to
drugs and alcohol to escape the horrors they experienced, or suffered
permanent physical damage from chemical agents used to destroy
crops and lands. Many, like Albert Lee Reynolds, lost their belief in
what they were fighting for.

We got the standard briefing, the one that was supposed to
convince us we were on some kind of a holy mission. Knights
crusading against the godless hordes of communism. I don't
think any of us believed what was being said. It was standard
government policy. . . . Something some jerk in Washington

dreamed up to justify his job. We were more sure than ever that what we were doing would have no beneficial effect on their [the Vietnamese] way of life.

While hundreds of thousands of teenagers were fighting in the jungles of Vietnam, hundreds of thousands of high school and college students were protesting the war on the streets of the United States. They marched in hundreds of demonstrations against the war and against the draft. They wore buttons that expressed their antiwar sentiment. "Make Love, Not War," was the most popular. Others said "Peace Now!" "Resist," and "Not with My Life You Don't." One of the earliest student declarations against the war read as follows:

Believing the United States participation in the war is a suppression of the Vietnamese struggle for national independence, we see no justification for our involvement. We agree with Senator Wayne Morse that "We should never have got in. We should never have stayed in. We should get out." Believing that we should not be asked to fight against the people . . . of Vietnam, we refuse to go.

Some students refused to register for the draft and were sent to prison. Others fled to Canada to escape military service. Some were beaten by adult supporters of the war. A small number of young soldiers in Vietnam sympathized with the peace demonstrations and wore the symbols of peace on their helmets. But many were enraged by the protests. Greg Lucso sent to the editor of his hometown paper an angry letter addressed to the protesters.

How the hell do you think we in Vietnam feel when we read of the dissension and unrest in our country caused by young, worthless radicals? This is what we feel like. We have an acute hatred, an unfathomable lust to maim, yes, even kill . . . all of you back in the World.

Many recruits in today's army see military service as a means of continuing their education and learning a profession or skill.

Since the Vietnam War, the United States has been very conservative in sending young men into battle. While troops fought in Kuwait against Iraq in 1991, and were used to restore order in various parts of the world, they were sent in cautiously and for a limited time.

Today, teenagers of both sexes join the armed forces not to fight, but to learn a skill or a profession. The army is no longer an end in itself but a means for a future career in civilian life. In a country where young people with a high school education are finding it increasingly difficult to find work, the military has become an important option for many. This is a major change from the days when young people attracted by patriotism and "the glory of war" often joined the military knowing the consequences of their decision.

SEX AND ROMANCE

In Puritan times, sexual relations between unmarried teenagers was strictly forbidden. Sex was for married couples only. Puritans tended to regard women as seducers whose beauty led men to destruction, much in the same way that Eve tempted Adam and led him to sin. Through poetry and sermons, ministers warned young girls that if they overemphasized their beauty, they could end up in hell. As one minister warned the young female members of his congregation, "Without holiness, your beauty is deformity, you are all over black and defiled, ugly and loathsome to all holy beings, and if you die in this condition, you'll be turned into hell with ugly demons, for eternity."

For men, seducing a young girl was a crime. A law was passed in Connecticut forbidding a young man to "insinuate into the affections of a young maiden by coming to them in places and seasons unknown to their parents for such." Adultery was a serious crime punishable by exile or the stocks.

By the eighteenth century, however, as Puritan influence declined, boys and girls mixed far more freely in America than in Europe. An English visitor was shocked to see both sexes go sleigh riding together. When a young man visited a young woman and her family, he was expected to stay overnight rather than travel a long distance home at night. Since most houses did not have guest rooms, he often "bundled" with her, that is, spent the night in the same bed with the girl he was

The Puritans were very strict about sexual relations before marriage, but at the same time were very frank in their discussions about sex.

visiting. The two were separated by a wooden board that was secured in the middle of the bed to separate them, and both of them slept with their clothes on. This was supposed to prevent sexual activity from taking place.

Many foreign visitors were shocked by this custom. Thomas Budley, a young visitor from England, was flabbergasted when the father of a household he was visiting invited him to bundle with his beautiful sixteen-year-old daughter, Jemima.

I was astonished at such a proposal and offered to set up all night when Jonathan immediately replied, "Oh you won't be the first man our daughter Jemima has bundled with, will it Jennie?" "No father, by many," Jenny replied, "but it will be the first Britisher." In this dilemma what could I do? I thought of the struggle with the passions of nature—to clasp Jemima in my arms and do what . . . ?

It seems that Thomas passed up the opportunity to bundle with Jemima in order to protect her honor, even though she seemed to feel it was not in any particular danger. While Thomas had his moral reservations, it became clear that many men and women found ways around the bundle boards. Throughout New England there were reports of children born seven months after the couple married. This was acceptable to the community as long as the husband and wife appeared in church and the husband confessed their sins.

The relaxation of sexual standards in the eighteenth century was only one indication that Puritan restrictions were weakening. An aristocracy and middle class had developed whose values were different from those of their Puritan forefathers. Young people of wealthy parents became less concerned with death and sin and more concerned with parties and pleasure. Even ten-year-old

Some Native-American tribes were as strict about sexual relations as the Puritans. Courtships were very elaborate rituals, and marriages were for life.

children dressed in fashionable clothes, went riding, played cards, and went to balls and masquerades. Girls of wealthy parents were trained to improve their appearance by learning to walk and sit with a perfectly straight back. They physically trained their backs by sitting in a stock with their hands and feet inserted through holes and bound, and their backs pressed against a wooden board. The goal in life for a young woman was to make herself look as beautiful as possible so she could marry well. The Puritans had seen this attitude developing a century earlier. In 1657, Ezekiel Rogers wrote to a minister, "I find greatest trouble and grief about the rising generation. . . . Even the children here and elsewhere make a woeful proof."

Many Native-American tribes were also very strict regarding sexual relations. They discouraged boys and girls from mixing before marriage and stressed that girls should be virgins until then. The Sioux

Black Elk, in his memoirs, described how a man went about courting a woman.

> In the old days, it was not so very easy to get a girl when you wanted to be married. Say I am a young man and I have seen a young girl who looks so beautiful to me that I feel all sick when I think about her. Maybe I hide by a spring where she sometimes goes to get water, and when she comes, I jump out and hold her and make her listen to me. If she likes me, I can tell that from the way she acts, for she is bashful and will not say a word or look at me the first time. So I let her go and then maybe I sneak around until I see her father alone, and I tell him how many horses I can give him for his beautiful girl, and by now I am feeling so sick I would give them all the horses in the world if I had them.

By the mid-nineteenth century, the American middle class was becoming stricter regarding sexual behavior. The latter part of the nineteenth century was known as the Victorian era. The age took its name from Queen Victoria of England, an extremely conservative monarch whose prudery and rigid morality set the tone for both English and U.S. middle-class society. Sex, which was discussed openly in the colonial world, was hidden in Victorian America. Teenage girls were supposed to pretend that sex did not exist. Even after they married, young girls were urged to avoid what one writer called "violent love" (sexual intercourse) and try to persuade their husbands to sleep in separate bedrooms, or at least in separate beds, in order to "avoid that freedom which degenerates into license." The author of one manual encouraged his young female reader to convince her husband that "conserving seminal fluid lifts him to a higher spiritual plane." All sorts of polite names were invented for body parts and bathroom activities. Toilet activities were called "natural functions," legs were limbs, childbirth was lying-in, and sexual organs were never referred to by any name. Sexual passion was considered a disease.

In the late nineteenth century, during the Victorian era, not only were sexual relations before marriage considered taboo, but Victorians did not even discuss or refer to anything sexual.

But the sin of sins for young people was masturbation. Boys were taught that "the solitary vice," as it was called, drove abusers insane, caused disease, blindness, cerebral palsy, impotence, and even death. Doctors warned young people that they could tell a person who had the "solitary vice" just by looking at him or her. One doctor wrote:

When I see a little girl or young lady, wasted and weak, with great hollow eyes and a sort of sullen tint on the haggard face, with the red hue of lips fled, the ears like white marble and the face covered with pimples, I know they have committed the sin which, if not checked, will lead them down to death.

Despite Victorian taboos, there were flirtations and even affairs, although a girl would be socially disgraced if her indiscretion were discovered.

The sexual urge was to be cured by cold baths, hard beds, and cutting down trees. Some parents handcuffed their children at night before they went to sleep. Children were given books with the titles *What Every Young Boy Should Know* and *What Every Young Girl Should Know.*

Girls were expected to be "pure." Premarital sex was absolutely forbidden. A girl who wasn't a virgin when she was married could be ostracized from the community if her "sin" was discovered. Eliza Southgate, a young woman of the nineteenth century, wrote in her diary, "Reputation undoubtedly is of great importance to all, but to a female, it's everything." Eliza felt she had strength of character to resist temptation until the right man came along. And if he didn't, "I have firmness enough to brave the sneer of the world and live an old maid if I never find the one I can love." She later found her ideal man but died in childbirth.

Among immigrant groups, where people lived packed together, and boys and girls mixed freely, there tended to be much sexual activity despite the overcrowding. They met on rooftops, in cellars, and behind stairs. Parents tried hard to maintain the old value systems of their native countries concerning the chastity of their daughters, but they were not always successful. Some young girls, faced with a choice between slave labor in a factory and relative comfort, even for a short while, in a life of prostitution, voluntarily chose the latter. Some girls were seduced by boys who then led them into a life of prostitution.

In the Jazz Age in the 1920s, women became more independent. One of the signs of the new freedom was, ironically, smoking.

While Victorian-era children grew up in a morally restricted society, their children did not. The period eventually gave way to the Jazz Age of the 1920s. It was a time of jazz, of course, and of prohibition (against the manufacture, transportation, and sale of alcoholic beverages). Because alcohol was illegal, individuals known as "bootleggers" appeared throughout the country illegally supplying liquor to clubs and individuals. In almost every city there were underground nightclubs called "speakeasies" where people could drink and dance. These establishments, with their promise of good times, fun, and excitement, attracted many young people. It also was the age of the "flappers," young women who wore their hair and skirts short, smoked, dressed in silk stockings, used cosmetics, danced the Charleston and the Black Bottom, and "petted" in the back seats of cars. (Petting was defined as any sexual activity short

The favorite dance of liberated women was the Charleston. During Prohibition, middle-class teenagers went to illegal clubs called "speakeasies" where they danced and drank.

of sexual intercourse.) The automobile provided a means of privacy and an opportunity for intimacy. While sexual activity was permissible, sexual intercourse—referred to as "going all the way"—was still considered taboo. A common expression of the times was "Nice girls don't."

During the Great Depression in the 1930s and World War II in the 1940s, sexual attitudes among teenagers changed once again. Life was too hard and serious for young people to think about having fun. Nor could many afford to go out on dates or to parties. There was a strong emphasis on female chastity. Many couples did not want to bring children into such a hard world. It was an era in which birth control methods were limited and abortion was illegal. Women who had abortions ran the risk of being severely injured or even dying at the hands of incompetent practitioners, many of whom were not even doctors. Some women refused to be married at a young age to avoid being burdened with a large number of children in those uncertain times. Even in the 1950s, as prosperity returned and society began to loosen up, this conservative attitude persisted. If a couple were having sexual relations, they would rarely admit it publicly.

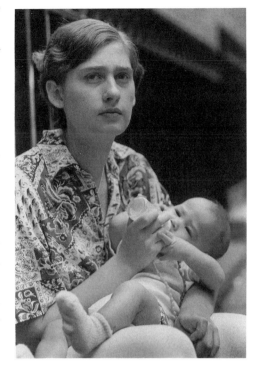

Being a teenage parent isn't easy.

Then in the 1960s, the sexual revolution exploded. With the introduction of contraceptive devices such as the pill, the legalizing of abortions, and a profound change in young people's attitudes brought about by the protest against the Vietnam War and the struggle for civil rights, teenagers became sexually active as never before. Couples lived together openly—often to the shock and dismay of their parents. Homosexuality, which in Puritan America could have been punished by death, and which was kept hidden throughout the nineteenth and most of the twentieth centuries, was suddenly brought out in the open.

Today, despite the recent "Safe Sex Campaigns" and the emphasis on abstinence, teenagers remain sexually active. Birth rates among unmarried teens continue to be high. In part because of the AIDS epidemic, homosexuals have become openly militant in demanding their full civil rights as well as the right to choose their own sexual lifestyles. Even though these rights have been seriously challenged with the specter of AIDS stalking the land, teenage sexual activity seems to be a permanent part of the youth culture.

Over 30 percent of high school students have had sexual intercourse by their fifteenth birthday. And each year, 2.5 million contract a sexually transmitted disease.

Peer pressure can be intense. Zaire, one of a group of New York and New Jersey teenagers interviewed by the *New York Times*, explained:

> My girlfriends tend to lose their virginity like 13, 14. They're doing it with 18, 19 year old boys. And they lose their virginity because they feel he's 18, he's 19 and I have to keep him. And you don't want to lose that, so these girls go out and put their lives in danger.

For some teenagers, having sex is one of the experiences that students must have before graduating, like taking the SATs. To graduate and still be a virgin is a mortifying state of affairs.

The fear of AIDS has, however, affected the thinking of many teenagers. According to Martha, a New Jersey high school student:

> A lot of boys are getting scared. They are starting to protect themselves and use condoms and they're starting to go to clinics on a regular basis. They're saying, like "I'm not sleeping with everything."

Rick confirms that this is what happened to him.

> When you see somebody who has AIDS, that'll blow you away. You'll be like, "Hold Up! Condom Time." Like Magic Johnson. Magic Johnson has been my idol because I love basketball. And when he caught AIDS I thought, wow even Mr. Indestructible caught it. I cried that day, oh man!

But there are always a number of students who believe themselves to be immortal and refuse to use any contraceptive. One student commented, "If any girl wants to sleep with me then she has to take me as I am or else she don't get me." He dismisses the idea that he will get a disease because he doesn't sleep with "those kind of girls."

In an attempt to minimize the risk, schools have tried to encourage students to practice safe sex and use contraceptive devices. They have even offered condoms to students. Whereas most students have accepted this policy calmly, some parents and church leaders are up in arms. They charge that by distributing condoms to boys and offering birth control devices like Norplant to girls, schools are encouraging sexual activity. One outraged minister commented, "You don't have to have a Ph.D. in child psychology to know that if you give a thirteen year old this kind of birth control, they will feel that you are sanctioning this kind of behavior."

Students often show reluctance to use the devices. Sometimes the reluctance is based on misinformation. Girls feel that if they use an implant, their hair will fall out, they'll develop cancer, or break out in rashes. In one survey, only 40 percent of students who were sexually active admitted using condoms 75 to 100 percent of the time.

Were our ancestors to enter a high school today, they would be shocked at the sexual experience teenagers have as well as the sex education that they have received. Puritans and Victorians alike were opposed to sexual relations before marriage, and both strongly condemned homosexuality. Today, this attitude persists in many areas of the country where religious values are still strict and strong. But for many young people, their concerns about premarital sex have more to do with physical consequences and less to do with moral or spiritual ones. Since the majority of students will have had sexual intercourse before graduating, the hope is that by making them aware of the potential dangers, they will modify their behavior and at least practice restraint, if not abstinence.

WORKING DAYS

I n colonial times, most children were expected to work at a young
age; their labor was expected to help their families. Young children
were given household chores by the time they were four or five. Girls
helped with cheesemaking, ironing, milling, sewing, dyeing, dipping
candles, and making soap. Boys did outdoor work, even if they went
to school. In their memoirs of growing up in New England, two
brothers, John and David Brainerd, recalled:

> The boy was taught that laziness was the worst form of origi-
> nal sin. He must rise early and make himself useful before he
> went to school, must be diligent there in his study, and
> promptly home to do chores at evening. His whole time out
> of school must be filled with some service such as bringing in
> fuel for the day, cutting potatoes for the sheep, feeding swine,
> watering the horses, picking berries. . . . He was expected
> never to be reluctant and not often tired.

Many colonial boys began their working careers by being "bonded"
to a farmer, merchant, or artisan as apprentices for a period of years in
order to learn a trade. Usually, the father was paid for his child's services. The master agreed to provide room, board, clothing, and some-

times a small amount of money, and to teach the boy a craft by which he could eventually make a living. Benjamin Franklin, one of this country's Founding Fathers, was once apprenticed to a printer and, in time, became publisher of his own newspaper. Many girls were apprenticed as domestic help, house servants, and farm laborers. At its best, the

In the eighteenth and early nineteenth centuries, young boys began their careers by working as apprentices in shops, where they learned a trade until they were ready to go out on their own.

apprentice system made it possible for children to learn a craft by which they could earn a living when they reached their late teens. While they worked, they were often protected by their families and the community from any abuse by the master.

For the children of the poor, it was a different story. They began their lives as indentured servants, which was little better than slave labor in many cases. Thousands of these children were orphans who had once lived on the streets of London and been shipped to America against their will. Upon arrival, they were bonded as indentured servants to craftsmen who paid the price of their passage. The children were forced to serve their masters until they were twenty-one, no matter how young they were when indentured. Without families to protect them, the children were often severely abused by their masters. They were made to work long hours and were poorly fed and sheltered.

One report on the death of a twelve-year-old apprentice read in part:

We do find that the body of John Walker was blackish and blue, the skin broken in diverse places, all his back with stripes given by his master Robert Latham; . . . also we found a bruise of his left arm and one of his left hip and one of his fingers frozen, and both of his heels frozen, his toes and the side of his foot frozen; . . . and that he did want sufficient food and clothing and lodging; . . . and that John was put forth in the extremity of cold; that in respect of cruelty and hard usage he died.

If working conditions were too bad, apprentices sometimes appealed to the courts, which, in cases of flagrant abuse, occasionally released them from their contracts. Others ran away. Newspapers of the time were filled with advertisements by masters seeking their runaway apprentices. One even put his search in the form of a poem.

> The present instant on the fourteenth day
> My apprentice boy did run away
> Thomas Sillinger he is called by name
> His indenture further testifies the same
> He has always been a vexatious lad
> One reason why he is so meanly clad.
>
> Of apple pies he took with him but five
> For to preserve himself alive
> Three quarter dollars are missed of late
> Which perhaps he took to pay his freight
> Believe him not if you be wise
> For he is very artful in telling lies.
> For which I whipt him I thought severe
> But did not make him shed one tear.

As bad as the indenture system was for some children, at least their period of service legally had to come to an end by the time they were twenty-one. Under slavery in the South, there was no release—except for death or flight. The African-American youth was bound to his or her master for life.

Slavery was introduced in America in the seventeenth century and lasted for more than two hundred years. While both northern and southern whites owned slaves at first, by the early nineteenth century slavery had been abolished throughout most of the North. In the South, where rice and cotton were grown on large plantations, slave labor was felt to be a necessity for white planters.

For African-American youth trapped in this vicious

African-Americans were brought to this country to provide the slave labor force for white planters. Children were made to work in the fields around the age of eight or nine and sometimes younger.

system, their labor belonged to their masters from the time they were old enough to work until they died. Slave labor was used for every job. African-Americans provided skilled labor as carpenters, masons, mechanics, shoemakers, boat builders. They worked inside the plantation house as servants and in the fields picking cotton and rice. Andrew Moss, who was a slave in the nineteenth century, recalled that his life as a worker began in childhood.

> I walked many a mile when I was a little feller, up and down the roes, following the grown folks. . . . I was nothin but a child endurin slavery, but I had to work de same as any man.

I went to de field and hoes cotton, pullin fodder and picked cotton with the rest of de hands. I kept up too, to keep from gettin any lashes when us got home at night.

Working in the fields was hard. Children had to clear the weeds away from the cotton while it was growing and then pick it once it was ripe. The sharp leaves would cut their fingers. Older children had to continuously stoop over to reach the cotton balls, straining their backs. They could be punished by the overseer if he felt they were not working fast enough. Any sign of resistance could trigger a brutal beating. When Frederick Douglass, who escaped from slavery and became a great national leader, was considered rebellious by his master, the seventeen-year-old was sent to William Covey, a "slave breaker," to be disciplined and made submissive. For six months the slave breaker beat Douglass day in and day out. He struck him with his fists, feet, and pieces of wood and whipped him with cowskins. He kept Douglass at hard work from sunup to sundown six days a week. Douglass was forced to labor in blazing heat and bitter cold, in rain and snow. Covey constantly spied on Douglass to make sure he never stopped working. He would sneak behind bushes to observe him or pretend to leave the house only to double-back and observe Douglass from his hiding place. Douglass never knew when Covey was watching him and when he was not. After six months of this torture, Douglass began to yield.

Mr. Covey succeeded in breaking me—in body, soul and spirit. My natural elasticity was crushed. My intellect languished. The disposition to read departed. . . . the dark night of slavery closed in on me and a man was transformed into a brute.

While Douglass eventually ran away to freedom in the North, and slavery came to end after the Civil War, another form of slavery—industrial slavery—was capturing America's children. Beginning in the

Children as young as nine worked in the mines. Many were killed in accidents or mine explosions.

late eighteenth century, the industrial revolution began in this country with the cotton industry. The first factory opened in Providence, Rhode Island, in 1791. By 1801, it employed over one hundred children between the ages of four and ten. Their main job was to remove and attach bobbins containing thread to the spindles. Their small, quick fingers were ideal for picking up and knotting broken threads. Tench Coxe, an apostle of the new industrialization, approvingly remarked that the children became "the little fingers . . . of the giant automatons of labor saving machinery."

By 1820, children formed almost half of the labor force of the New England mills. The owners boasted how profitable it was for them to use child labor and justified their greed by claiming that it was morally edifying for children to work. Otherwise they would become part of the poor, idle, and vicious elements of society. Josiah Quincy, an inhabitant of New England, visited a plant in 1801. He was shocked at what he saw.

[I] pity those little creatures plying in a contracted [narrow] room, among flyers and cogs [machinery] when nature requires for them air, space, sports. There is a dull dejection in the countenance of all of them.

The more the United States industrialized, the more it depended on child labor. Children worked in factories, mills, mines, department stores, telegraph industries, laundries . . . no industry was exempt. A caramel factory in Chicago employed over two hundred children, most of whom were girls who sat at long tables wrapping and packing caramels. They were paid by the piece and earned pennies a day. During the Christmas season, they worked from seven in the morning to nine at night with twenty minutes for lunch and no supper—a ninety-six-hour week. In the coal mining areas of Pennsylvania, Illinois, and West Virginia, children began work in the mines at the age of seven. They began by separating slate from the coal on the outside of the mine. By the time they were ten, they were working inside. They inhaled coal dust, which ruined their lungs, and sometimes died in the mine disasters when gas exploded, trapping those below.

These children were a new breed of workers. Under the old apprentice system, children learned a trade or acquired work experience that would enable them as adults to set up their own business or work for others at a reasonable wage. Factory and mine work had no future for children. Nor did it allow them time for education. Despite laws to the contrary, many mill owners provided only minimal or no education for children. But even if there were classes, children were often too tired to attend after their working day. Harriet Robinson was ten years old when she went to work in a clothing mill in nineteenth-century New England. For her, the hardest part of the job was the long hours children were forced to work.

The working hours of all the girls extended from five o'clock in the morning until seven in the evening with one half hour for breakfast and dinner. Even the doffers [young girls who

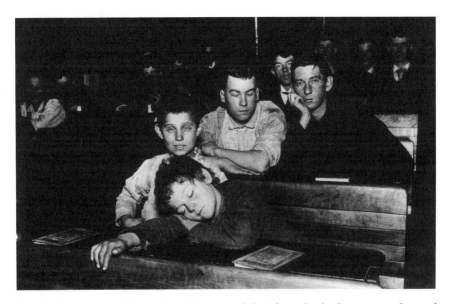

Because so many children worked late at night after school, they were exhausted during the day and had trouble keeping awake in class.

removed the full bobbins containing the spun cloth and re-placed it with an empty one] were forced to be on duty 14 hours a day, and this was the greatest hardship on the lives of these children.

Children were used to operate complicated machinery at which they worked long hours. Irene Ashby, a visitor from England, saw six- and seven-year-olds working twelve hours a day. Some worked at night and were kept awake by the superintendent throwing cold water on their faces. Ashby asked a little girl of eight what she did when she was very tired. "I cry," the child responded.

The jobs were often as dangerous as they were long. An anonymous fourteen-year-old girl described her first day of work to an interviewer.

As I stood looking at all the different wheels turning this way and that, it looked like a jig saw to me. I was scared to death watching girls place their hands on different parts of the machine. The machines frightened me so much that the girl who was teaching me told the foremen I was too young to do the work and too small a child to be put on the machines.

Thirteen-year-old Al Priddy worked in the New England mill. His job was to clean a dangerous piece of machinery, which, by law, had to be stopped before it could be cleaned. But none of the men whose work depended on the machine could afford to have it turned off. So Al had to clean it while it was in motion.

I had to clean fallers, which, like teeth, chopped on one's hand, unless great speed and precautions were used. I stuck a hand brush into swift-turning pulleys and brushed the cotton off; I dodged past the mules and iron posts they met just in time to avoid being crushed. Alfred Skinner, a close friend of mine had his body crushed badly. In cleaning the wheels [the] cotton waste would lump and I would risk my life and fingers to extract the waste in time.

Many children were injured by the machines and lost fingers or a hand. They inhaled small particles of lint, which eventually scarred their lungs, or they contracted tuberculosis from working in a dirty environment without ventilation.

City children, most of whose parents were immigrants, were able to work outside the factory. They found jobs as errand boys, messengers, butcher's assistants, and vendors selling merchandise on the street: gum, candy, shoelaces, pencils, cookies. Finding a job wasn't always easy. One boy explained:

I rose at six-thirty each morning and was out stamping the streets at seven. There were always hundreds of jobs, but thousands of boys clutching after them. The city was swarming with these boys, aimless, bewildered and as hungry for work as I was.

The most desired job was that of a "newsie" (newsboy). Before 1920, newspapers relied on children for over 50 percent of their circulation. After school was out, children, usually between the ages of eleven and fifteen, worked from afternoon to evening selling newspapers on the streets. They were their own bosses. They sought customers from late afternoon to late at night. They planted themselves on street corners, in front of subways, department

One of the favorite jobs of city children in the slums was that of newsie—newsboy or newsgirl.

stores, groceries, bridges, ferry landings, and tunnels.

The newsies came from every ethnic group, but most of them were from working-class families. Girls as well as boys sold newspapers, although boys outnumbered them. Newsies enjoyed their work. The job gave them freedom from adult supervision, the company of their peers, a chance to earn money and have fun. Many worked until the early hours of the morning because they wanted to and because they earned more money that way. At the same time, many newsies were "street children" who had no place to live. They sold newspapers to earn a living, slept in hallways, in the subway, wherever they could find a spot to keep warm and not be disturbed by the police.

One of the most famous events in New York City's history was the newsies' strike of 1899. When two newspapers tried to double-cross the newsies by changing the price scale, they found themselves with a strike on their hands. Throughout the city, all newsies refused to sell either of the two papers. Despite racial and ethnic differences, they were unified in this effort. Black and white, Irish, Jewish, and Italian newsboys and -girls worked together. They carried signs reading "Please Don't Buy the *World* or the *Herald*." "Help the Newsboys. Our Cause Is Just." When one of the other newspapers asked a newsboy why he was striking, he proclaimed, "We're here for our rights and we will die defending them." When a truck tried to load a bunch of newspaper, about a hundred boys gathered and showered it with stones. When another fleet of trucks tried to deliver papers to a group of distributors, about five hundred boys gathered. A local newspaper described what happened: "They formed a circle and as fast as any man got his bundle of papers and tried to get away with him, they swept down upon him with cries of 'kill the scab!,' mauled him till he dropped his papers and ran, and then tore the sheets into small bits and trampled them in the mud."

By the end of the second week, the newspapers realized they had been beaten. They offered a compromise that was accepted by the newsies, and the strike was over. Their victory served as an inspiration for newsboys and -girls throughout the country. Strikes sporadically broke out whenever newspapers violated their agreements. Many of these strikes were won.

While working boys were expected to be street smart, tough, daring, and pushy, all these traits were forbidden to girls. Parents felt that their daughters had to be protected from the streets. The ultimate fear of parents was that their daughters would be assaulted or seduced into a life of prostitution. Girls did sell newspapers and candy, gum, and flowers on the streets, and helped sell goods on pushcarts. But often they were under the protective eye of an older brother. Because women were paid less than men and worked equally as hard, if not harder, there was always the danger of falling into a life of prostitution if they lost their jobs.

But even if a girl did not have to work on the streets like her brothers, this did not mean she was free from work. Girls watched younger children and helped with "womanly" tasks such as cooking, cleaning, shopping for groceries—all of which were designed to prepare them for their future role as wives and mothers. Whenever there was a boarder (many families took in boarders to earn extra money), it was the girls who cleaned and cooked for the tenants. Girls also hired out as domestic help, working as maids, cleaning girls, and cooks. Some worked in department stores, selling goods to customers and receiving as little as $2.50 a week.

One of the hardest jobs was sewing. Many homes were sweatshops, and it was a common sight to see the whole family seated together around a table, a pile of unfinished clothes in the middle, sewing from before dawn to late at night. While some boys might escape to a job in the street, girls were more likely to be trapped. Even going to school did not exempt a girl from doing her share. An eleven-year-old girl who made artificial flowers after school described her day.

> Every morning before school, I sweep out three rooms and help get breakfast. Then I wash dishes. In the mornings, on the way to school, I leave finished flowers at the shop and stop for more work on the way home. After school, I do homework for an hour, then I make flowers. All of us, my sisters, my cousins and my aunts, my mother work on flowers. We put the yellow centers into the forget-me-nots. It takes me an hour to finish over one gross and I make three cents for that. If we all work all our spare time we can make as much as two dollars between us.

By 1912, public opinion began to turn against child labor. A series of magazine and newspaper articles appeared throughout the country exposing its evils. Photographs taken by crusading photographers such as Lewis Hine and Jacob Riis documented the horrors of child labor in factories and slums. States began to pass child labor laws, limiting the number of hours a child could work and setting a minimum age.

Factory owners struck back. They criticized federal interference with their right to make money. When Congress passed a law regulating child labor, the Supreme Court overturned it. When an attempt was made to pass a congressional amendment protecting children, it was defeated. Not until 1941 did the U.S. Supreme Court validate the right of Congress to regulate child labor.

However, there was one group of children neglected by the new legislation. Farm children continued to suffer from brutal working conditions. Ned Cobb was raised on a farm in rural Alabama and was expected to do a man's work by the time he was nine.

My daddy put me to plowin the first time at nine years old. He had two mules and he had me to plow in one and him plowin the other. And I had to plow barefooted on that rocky country anything liable to skin up my feet. That year the weather was dry . . . and, doggone it, the gnats would eat me up and I was just nine years old. So I would fight the gnats and my daddy got mad with me for that . . . and he picked me up by the arm and he held me up and nearly wore out a switch on me. That was the first whippin he ever give me bout plowin. I wasn't big enough for the job, that's the truth. He had me in the field doin' a man's work and I was a little boy.

In the 1920s, an increasing number of children began to work with their families as migrant farm labor. Until the Great Depression began in 1929, many of the migrant workers were Mexican. In the 1930s, they were joined by farmers from the Southwest who had lost their farms because of drought and low prices. Cesar Chavez, whose father had lost his land during the crash, was one of the children who joined the huge labor force of migratory workers that followed the crops in the 1930s. They picked everything that grew in California, including cotton, fruits, and vegetables. Cesar worked alongside his parents from "can see to can't see," sunrise to sunset, in temperatures that often

Farm children's lives were extremely hard. In the cotton fields for example, they began working as young as six or seven. By the time they were teenagers, they were sometimes picking more than a hundred pounds of cotton a day.

exceeded one hundred degrees. The family lived in miserable camps with poor food.

By 1935, over two million children, 20 percent of the youth population under eighteen, were working, many of them at extremely low paying jobs. One girl remembered stringing safety pins on a wire with her family for a total sum for the whole family of three dollars a week. Another made doll's dresses.

> I got home at 3:30 from school and sat down and worked at the kitchen table making doll's dresses. We had dinner at 5:00 and afterwards I worked from six to nine when it was time to go to bed. My two brothers worked alongside of me. My job was cutting threads. I did this everyday for years. It didn't matter if it was raining or the sun was shining, light or dark out. We had to work long hours because the pay was so little. I thought I would go crazy, the work was so tedious.

While it was difficult for whites to find work, it was even harder for blacks. Many blacks who held jobs were forced to surrender them to whites. In Alabama, whites ambushed and killed black railroad workers when they refused to step down. Jobs that whites had once considered beneath them as "nigger work" they now eagerly sought. Over 50 percent of black males were out of work, compared with 39 percent of white males. Frank Johnson, an African-American, quit school to work, even though he was an honor student and had hoped to go to college.

> My family could hardly pay the rent or buy food. So I quit school to find work. I got a job delivering milk in the morning. I used to get food that way, drinking what was ever left over. I worked as a pinboy in a bowling alley. Eventually, I got a job as an elevator boy in a department store. I was determined to find work even if it meant having several jobs at once and working 15 to 16 hours a day. All of it was marginal. None of it had a future. I don't know what would have happened to me if I continued down this path.

Despite the efforts of children to find jobs, some four million who sought work remained unemployed. For the first time in the nation's history, the federal government created jobs for older youths through the Civilian Conservation Corps (CCC) and the National Youth Administration (NYA). Young men who joined the CCC (women were not eligible) went to work building roads, dams, and bridges and restoring forests on federal land. They lived in camps that were run in a military style, and the teenagers wore army uniforms, although they did not train for combat. The NYA taught job skills and found employment for thousands of teenagers of both sexes.

But the problem of youth employment was not solved until World War II. During the war, millions of teenagers joined the military, while those too young to serve easily found part-time jobs. There was no longer any need for children to work as slave labor in factories.

Women were hired to replace male factory workers who had gone to war. Family incomes for middle-class families were sufficient to support a family without children having to work. Even children from poor families could go to school instead of working. The one group of children who did not benefit from the economic changes brought by the war were those whose families worked on farms or were migrant workers. Another forty years would pass before they received some protection from exploitation.

During the Great Depression, many Mexican children worked as migrant laborers, traveling around from farm to farm picking fruit and vegetables as the crops were ready for harvest.

In the postwar years, strong legislation protecting children from exploitation, combined with a booming economy, freed most children in the United States from the necessity of work. But beginning in the 1970s, a new problem arose. An increasing number of youth from poor families who graduated high school could not find jobs. A recent study in the Harlem section of New York showed that for every $4.25-an-hour job that opens up in a McDonald's-type fast-food restaurant, there are fourteen applications. Fewer part-time jobs are available, and more and more graduates are finding it hard to find full-time jobs after graduation. Unemployment in some black communities is already over 50 percent. In 1994, only 10.6 percent of black students and 14.6 percent of Hispanic students between the ages of sixteen and nineteen had jobs, compared with almost 20 percent of white students the same age. Enrico, a sixteen-year-old dropout, complained about the situation: "We go to school and get an education for nothing, for nothing. They

In order to prevent young people from dropping out of school, new programs have been introduced that teach students skills they can use in today's workplace.

[whites] don't want us to be educated, they don't want us to compete with them for jobs." In a society that has lost several million manufacturing and factory jobs, and replaced some of them with jobs requiring sophisticated technical and communication skills, many young people find they cannot compete. Federal programs like the Job Corps were set up to train disadvantaged youth, but in the past few decades, the unemployment rates for minority and poor teenagers have risen to as much as 50 percent.

In some ways, we have gone from one bad situation to another. In the past, there was a great demand for young workers because they could be underpaid and overworked. Today, young people find themselves without jobs of any kind, let alone meaningful work, their skills and talents wasted. As young people continue to be unemployed in large numbers, work begins to lose its value. The netherworld of drug dealing and crime appears more attractive. This is a problem that many experts predict will grow worse in the coming years.

6

HATE THY NEIGHBOR

"Bigotry," one African-American militant once said, "is as American as cherry pie." Ever since the first Africans were brought to this country as slaves, European whites were highly prejudiced against them. Not only did whites maintain an almost absolute power of life and death over blacks, but they tried to morally justify slavery as being sanctioned by God for the benefit of the slaves. White children growing up in the South before the Civil War were taught never to question slavery. Louise Clark Pyrnelle wrote her autobiography *(Diddie, Dumps and Tot)* "to tell of the pleasant and happy relations that existed between master and slave."

As a child, Louise and her sisters played games, rode horses, and listened to stories told by faithful black servants who had names like Mammy and Snake Bite Jim and Uncle Sambo. She claimed all the servants loved and protected the children and were loved by them as well. The girls loved their Mammy, who had also nursed their mother, best of all. The children also had three black children for servants who "belonged" to them and were in training to be their maids. They regarded black children as toys to play with. During one holiday season, Louise remembered asking her parents for some playmates.

"Mamma, being this is Christmas, could we have some of the quarter niggers to go to the house and play injuns with us?"

Each of the children were told that they might select one of the little Negroes to play with her. Diddie took a little mulatto girl named Agnes, Dumps selected Frances, a lively little darkey who could dance and pat and sing and shout. Tot took Polly, a big girl of 14.

If it was "fun" for white children to be able to pick and choose black children for servants, it could be quite a burden for black children. In one slave family, a black child was warmed by the fire and then laid crosswise at the bottom of the bed to keep the feet of the master and his wife warm. One parent gave his son a black "play child," whom he instructed as follows: "I give your young master over to you and if you let him hurt himself, I'll pull your ears; if you let him cry, I'll pull your ears; if he wants anything and you don't let him have it, I'll pull your ears."

Frederick Douglass began life as a slave and became the foremost African-American leader in the nineteenth century.

For the young Frederick Douglass, who was a slave throughout his childhood, the worst part was the despair he felt. Douglass recalled that the constant physical and psychological abuse he suffered continually reminded him that there was no hope for a better life under slavery. "The over-work and the brutal chastisements combined with the ever gnawing and soul devouring thought . . . 'I am a slave, a slave for life—a slave with no rational ground to hope for freedom'—rendered me a living embodiment of physical and mental wretchedness."

As noted earlier, Douglass escaped from slavery and won wide respect in the North for being an eloquent and articulate spokesman against slavery. But as far as most white Americans were concerned, it made no difference if a black person were slave or free. Throughout the nineteenth and twentieth centuries, gangs of northern whites, most of which were composed of immigrant teenagers, periodically terrorized blacks. In the 1830s, they burned down an orphanage for African-American children in New York and went on a rampage against them in Boston and Philadelphia. Only in Massachusetts were children of both races permitted to attend the same school. But while that enabled many black children to get a better education, it did not result in any widespread acceptance. Charlotte Foster, an African-American teenager who attended a Boston school before the Civil War, angrily wrote that her so-called friends in class snubbed her when they met on the street, causing her great pain.

> Oh it is hard to go through life meeting contempt with contempt, hatred with hatred, fearing, with good reason to love and trust anyone whose skin is white. On the bitter, passionate feelings of my soul again there rises the question, "When will this cease? Is there no help? How long must we continue to suffer?"

Thirteen-year-old Walter White was accompanying his father, a postman, on his mail delivery rounds in Atlanta, Georgia, on September 22, 1906, when a race riot exploded. White and his father returned home, prepared to defend their family and property from the mob that was headed in their direction. With guns in hand, father and son waited inside the dark house. When the mob appeared, White heard the son of a grocer with whom his family had traded for many years yell, "That's where the nigger mail carrier lives! Let's burn it down.

Until the 1960s, African-Americans in the South were segregated from whites. When going to a movie theater, they were forced to use a separate entrance and sit in the balcony.

It's too nice for a nigger to live in!" Walter White's father turned to him.

> In a voice as quiet as if he was asking me to pass the sugar, he said, "Son, don't shoot until the first man puts his foot on the lawn and then—don't you miss!" In that instant there opened up in me a great awareness. I knew then who I was. I was a negro . . . a person to be hunted, hanged, abused, discriminated against, kept in poverty and ignorance. It made no difference how intelligent, or talented, my millions of brother[s] and I were nor how virtuously we lived. A curse like that of Judas was on us.

Racial prejudice against Native Americans was almost as intense as the prejudice against African-Americans. No one feared Indians

One of the worst consequences of segregation was that many children were denied the opportunity to escape poverty and make a better life for themselves than that of their parents.

more than the children of white settlers who traveled through the West during pioneer days. In their diaries and letters, they repeated all the stereotypes they had heard from their parents. Indians were "dirty," "sneaky," "thievin," "untrustworthy," "liars." Many parents used Indians to scare their children by warning them, "If you're not good, the Injuns will get you." Some fantasized about being kidnapped, tortured, scalped, and eaten by wild savages. A few children were given poison by their parents to carry in lockets, which they were instructed to swallow if they were taken prisoner by Indians. Anne Ellis, who had long yellow hair as a child, remembered her mother scaring her so much about Indians that she had nightmares about being attacked. "I have felt him [an Indian] lift my scalp from my head and seen it dangling from his belt."

Indians rarely attacked wagon trains. When they appeared, it was usually to trade. However, many pioneer children had been so frightened by their parents' stories that they would hide until the traders were gone. Mary Todd, who shared similar fears, eventually learned to put things in perspective as a result of her father's guidance.

> Bands of Indians occasionally passed us. Some were painted up in war paint, also having Eagle feather headdresses. We children thought they looked frightful. They would gallop right up to us saying, "Me go fight Crows." Thus they let us know they were friendly to whites. At night . . . when the wolves lifted up their voices and howled, I would think of those hideous looking Indians and the stories I heard of their treachery until I seemed to see the wily creatures sneaking up to our camp. . . . My father always tried to calm my fears. He told us that all this country really belonged to the Indians and that the white people were crowding them out by killing the buffalo and taking their lands. We then felt more kindly to them.

Some of the bolder and more curious children put aside their fears and learned about the Indians. They wandered into tents to see how they lived. Other children were aided by them. Eleven-year-old Elisha Brooks was on his way to California with his mother and five brothers and sisters when they were deserted by their driver. They wandered around lost until they encountered a band of Sioux. The Sioux offered to help. Terrified at first, Elisha reluctantly gave up some of his prejudice. "They were not so bad as they were painted," he said.

Native-American children were as fearful of whites as whites were fearful of them. When Black Elk, an Ogalala Sioux, was growing up in the mid-nineteenth century, his grandmother would discipline him by saying, "If you are not good the Wasichus [whites] will get you." Sara Winnemucca, a Paiute, was terrified of whites as a child.

> Oh what a fright we got when we heard white people were coming. Everyone ran as fast as they could. . . . My poor

mother was carrying my little sister on her back and trying to make me run but I was so frightened I could hardly move my feet. My aunt said to my mother, "Let us bury our girls or we shall all be killed and eaten up." They went to work and buried us and told us if we made any noise or cried out, they would surely come and eat us. So our mother buried me and my cousin; planted some sage brush over our faces to keep the sun from burning them and we were left there all day.

Eventually Sara Winnemucca had direct contact with whites when they visited her grandfather's lodging. It was a shocking experience.

Just then I peeped around my mother to see them. I gave a scream and said, "Oh, they are like owls." . . . I only saw their big white eyes and I thought then that their faces were all hair. I imagined I could see their white eyes all night long.

Lame Deer, a Lakota Sioux, had similar impressions of whites as bearded owls.

I had never seen so much hair on a man. It covered all of his face and grew down to his chest. It made him look like a mattress comes to life. He had eyes of a dead owl . . . a washed-out, blue-green hue.

Unfortunately, the tribes had more reason to fear the whites than the whites them. The settlers, supported by the army, were destroying the way of life of the Native Americans, and although both sides committed atrocities, white soldiers systematically slaughtered whole villages of Indians, including women and children.

At the same time that Native-American culture was being destroyed, a new urban subculture was being created in the cities by immigrant groups from Europe. Italians, Jews, and eastern Europeans joined the Irish and Germans, bringing with them not only their new hopes but their old prejudices. These prejudices were passed on to their children. Many of these animosities spilled over into ethnic and racial gang wars. Irish, Jews, Italians, and blacks fought each other constantly, using racial or ethnic epithets as they battled. The words *dago, kike, mick,* and *nigger* flew as fast and furious as the bottles and stones that were thrown. When Mike Gold crossed into an Italian neighborhood and was caught, the gang leader was overjoyed.

> "Horray a Jew, a Jew," he screamed. He slugged me with his stick. The others yelled and joined in the slugging. Down Mulberry Street I ran. They pursued me throwing sticks and stones, bricks and vegetables. "Christ killer," someone yelled. A stone caught me in the temple and I tasted blood on my lips. A brick caught my right shin. My ribs were bruised by the sticks. My shirt was slimy with horse dung and rotten vegetables.

But ethnic and religious prejudice, as fierce as it could be at times, never reached the degree of murderous rage that racial prejudice did. African-Americans and Native Americans were not the only people to suffer. When Chinese and Japanese immigrants arrived in California in the nineteenth century, they were greeted with violence and hatred by whites. There was so much hostility against them that by the turn of the twentieth century, laws had been passed that virtually excluded them from immigrating to the United States.

Despite the restrictions, a small number of Japanese were able to establish families here in the twentieth century. Although there was always strong prejudice against them, it was not until Japan attacked the United States on December 7, 1941, that the prejudice escalated. Tom Kaizawa was twelve and had just come from a Buddhist religious service when the attack came.

> Someone called out, "Attack!" "Attack!" "Japan bombed Pearl Harbor." "Lot of people dead." I was frightened. My friends

were scared too. As I neared my house, I saw my neighbors huddled with my mother. They looked tense and worried. . . . I heard a man's voice say "Yellow Japs." The words stunned me. In that instant, I realized everything had changed. Japan, which had been such a strong influence on my life, was now the enemy. I churned with anger and shame that a nation of people related to me had done something so horrible. I felt betrayed.

While there was a great deal of hostility toward Japanese-American students, some of their fellow white students and teachers insisted that they be considered as Americans. A high school student remembered how his teacher had pleaded with the students not to blame the American-born Japanese for the war. One youth reported:

> The following day [after the bombing of Pearl Harbor] I had to go to school and I really hated to go. I had a feeling that everyone would accuse me for the treachery of the Japanese forces. I was afraid that my classmates would regard me as one of their enemies. I was astonished when the fellows talked to me as an American and how the war would affect us Americans.

On February 19, 1942, President Franklin Delano Roosevelt, caving in to the racial prejudice against the Japanese Americans and Japanese residents, signed an executive order relocating them to detention centers. Their lands and property were confiscated. Almost everyone lost their homes and businesses, many of which were snapped up by whites eager to take advantage of their misfortunes. Children reported having rocks thrown at them. Vigilantes roamed the streets and buildings, and homes were burned down. By August of 1942, over one hundred thousand Japanese were rounded up and shipped to concentration camps; 60 percent of them were American born and thus deprived of their constitutional rights as citizens. Many thought they were going

During World War II, Japanese Americans were forced to live in concentration camps such as this. They had done nothing against the government but were interred because of the prejudice against them.

to mass executions. Parents lived in rooms that were twelve feet by twelve feet with one lightbulb, two cots, and a cast-iron stove, while their children lived in separate rooms nearby. The camps, located in California and some other western locations, were in miserable locations. One young man who was interned remembered his camp at Manzanar.

> The desert was bad enough. The mushroom barracks made it worse. The constant cyclonic storms loaded with sand and dust made it even worse. After living in well-furnished homes with modern conveniences, and suddenly forced to live the life of a dog, is something one cannot readily forget.

The camps were not like those in Nazi Germany or Japan. People were not tortured or systematically beaten and brutalized. Families were not broken up; children were not taken from their parents. But they were surrounded with guards, barbed wire, and, at times, subjugated to harassment and occasional violence by the government. One man was shot by a sentry for no apparent reason except that the guard was irritated about something he did. An elderly man was shot and killed because he wandered outside the restricted area to pick flowers. A group of children were arrested for sleigh riding on a hill outside the compound.

In an effort to compensate for feelings of inferiority some Japanese children would speak only English. When one girl refused, her friends stopped talking to her. American movie stars became the idols of Japanese teens. One young girl complained that her figure was not like Lana Turner's, one of the sexier stars of the day. Some children resented being Japanese and tried to make friends with whites whenever they could make contact. One girl reported that she hated having a "Japanese face." Others blamed their parents.

> Father you have wronged me grievously
> I know not why you punished me.
> For sins not done nor reasons known
> You have caused me misery.

Young people tried to live normal lives in the camps as best they could. They went to school, played sports, had dances, and went out on dates. Girls and boys worried a good deal about dating. One girl complained she was not meeting enough boys because she had to work all day. But in general, the traditional distance between boys and girls began to break down. Normally, Japanese families were very protective of their daughters. It was considered a disgrace if a girl had sexual relations before marriage. Now some young woman had affairs.

Life in the camps was often marked with apathy, boredom, outbursts of violence, divisions between groups, and conflicts with the army. A major crisis developed when the U.S. government decided to require everyone to sign a document that determined their loyalty. Two questions that infuriated many young Japanese and Japanese-American young men were whether they would serve in the U.S. military and whether they would renounce loyalty to Japan. Some children,

Japanese-American families were forced to give up their homes and settle in the camps, even though most were American citizens.

who were more assimilated, were not opposed to saying yes to both questions. Other teenagers were furious. Many young men answered no to both questions—not because they were disloyal but because they were hurt and angry at the way they were treated. One teenager told authorities: "At one time I said I was willing to die for this country. That's the way I felt. But now I've changed my mind. You Caucasian Americans should realize I got a raw deal."

The tensions led to young people forming gangs and defying authorities. Some called strikes to complain about low wages, mistreatment, and unjust imprisonment or transfer of protesters. Other gangs defiantly proclaimed their loyalty to Japan and even carried out ceremonies pledging allegiance to the emperor. The gangs intimidated others into joining. Once a person joined, there was no way of leaving without the risk of being beaten up and harassed.

It was not until the war was over that the Japanese were finally allowed to leave the camps. Many young men did serve with distinction in the United States Army. But it would still take another thirty-five years before they would be compensated for the property they lost.

Other groups suffered from prejudice during World War II. A number of religious groups like the Jehovah's Witnesses, Amish, and Mennonites were against war on religious grounds. Many men went to jail or were beaten by mobs for their pacifism. Their children were taunted with charges of being Nazis. The children also suffered because their religion forbid them to salute the flag of any country.

Inside the concentration camps, young people tried to make as normal a life for themselves as possible. Many attended school, and some young men even enlisted in the army.

Wanda Davis remembered how she refused to salute the U.S. flag in class until her teacher forced her to do so by threatening to paddle her. When she told her mother she had yielded and asked what she should do, her mother replied, "Pray to God for forgiveness."

European Jews were Adolf Hitler's main victims, and Jews in the United States were blamed by some Americans for pushing the United States to enter the war. Jewish children had long suffered from anti-Semitism in this country. They were often called Christ killers, kikes, and sheenies. Gangs of Christian children attacked Jewish children and painted swastikas on their houses and sometimes destroyed their property.

Latino people also suffered from racial prejudice because of their dark skins. Many had immigrated to the United States to work in the fields as migrant labor. Because their skins were dark and they were poor, many whites treated them as they treated blacks. Cesar Chavez, who would become a labor leader of migrant workers, experienced such prejudice as a youth. To earn extra money, Cesar, son of a Mexican-American migrant worker, had a job in a nearby town shining shoes on Saturdays. The police would not let him enter the town unless he was carrying a shoe-shine box because Mexicans were not allowed to visit or even shop there. Most small restaurants carried signs that said "White Trade Only." Cesar and his friend made the mistake of entering a restaurant to buy hamburgers.

> There was this young waitress. And there was this familiar sign again. She looked up at us and she sort of—it wasn't what she said, it was just a gesture. A gesture of total rejection. She said, "Wattyawant?" So we told her we'd like to buy two hamburgers. She sort of laughed a sarcastic laugh. And she said, "Oh we don't sell to Mexicans. Why don't you go across to a Mexican town. You can buy them over there." And she never knew how much she was hurting us. But it stayed with us.

In an attempt to overcome prejudice, some Mexican parents tried to Americanize their children. They warned them not to speak Spanish. "Don't speak that ugly language, you are an American now," one girl was told by her sister. Many were denied opportunities because of racial prejudice. Julia Luna, who had ambitions to work in an office, was told by her typing teacher, "Who's going to hire you, you're so dark?" During World War II, U.S. soldiers rioted against Mexican youth living in Los Angeles because they were wearing "zoot suits," which consisted of a long draped coat, high-waisted pants with baggy legs and pegged cuffs, a key chain, and "porkpie" hat. Racist whites irrationally saw this practice as a threat to their values and tried to suppress it through violence. Laws were passed in Los Angeles against dressing in zoot suits, and when mobs attacked Hispanic youths wear-

In recent times Muslims have become the target for prejudice, especially when incidents such as a bombing occur.

ing them, the Latino teenagers were arrested, not members of the attacking mob.

In the late 1950s, the first mass attack on prejudice occurred in the South when African-Americans launched a direct assault on segregation. As the walls of legal separation came tumbling down, and whites reluctantly began to enter into a serious dialogue with blacks, the barriers that prevented African-Americans from succeeding in U.S. society were gradually removed.

The militancy of the civil rights movement of the 1960s encouraged others to assert their rights. Women protested against being second-class citizens in the workplace and in society. They refused to accept lower pay than men for the same work or being passed over for promotions because they were women. More recently, they have spoken out against sexual harassment. Native Americans have asserted their rights in an effort to correct past injustices. They have successfully sued for the return of lands taken away from them and have regained exclusive fishing and hunting rights to their territories. They have also won the right to establish gambling casinos on their property, a mixed blessing that has caused serious problems in some communities and benefited others. Homosexuals, who have been continually victimized by "gay bashing," attacked by gangs of hostile youth, and harassed by the police, also revolted in the 1960s and became militant and outspoken. This crusade intensified in recent times as a result of the AIDS crisis, the terrible toll it has taken on the homosexual community, and the hostility it has generated. Reflecting the new spirit of the age, laws were passed on both federal and state levels forbidding discrimination in almost every area of public life.

But despite the efforts of the past thirty years, prejudice against African-Americans, Native Americans, Jews, women, homosexuals, Latinos, and Asians remains strong among large sections of young people. On the extreme right, groups like the skinheads glorify violence against minorities. Daily, there are hundreds, if not thousands, of incidents involving prejudice, few of which make the headlines. In a high school in Connecticut, a group of senior white students wrote a coded message in their yearbook that spelled out "Kill all niggers!" They were not allowed to attend graduation ceremony, but they were given their diplomas. In Mississippi, a supervisor tried to discourage an interracial couple from attending the senior prom. He suggested to the girl, who was African-American, that it would have been better if she had not been born. Black students organized their own prom in protest. In Texas, a judge threatened to place the daughter of a Hispanic woman in a foster home if her mother did not stop speaking Spanish to her at home. He modified his threat when the Hispanic community loudly protested against his prejudice. And at the Citadel in South Carolina, a military academy similar to West Point, male students made life so difficult for the first female cadet accepted to the school, that she felt forced to quit.

According to the most recent statistics, 60 percent of the seven thousand incidents of bias reported by the FBI were motivated by racial prejudice against whites, blacks, or Native Americans. While mass prejudice against Jews and Catholics has diminished, it has not disappeared. Eighteen percent of bias cases were against Catholics and

Jews. Twelve percent were against homosexuals. These figures, however, represent the tip of the iceberg because most incidents do not get reported. Nor do the tens of thousands of daily insults that are inflicted on minorities of all kinds. If the American people have put the worst of their prejudiced behavior behind them, they still have a long way to go before wiping it out completely.

7

THE STRUGGLE TO LEARN

The Puritans introduced public education in America. While the majority of children did not go to schools, most Puritan children received some education. Parents usually taught their children the alphabet and how to read and write. Rich parents either had tutors for their children or sent them to private schools. Free schools were non-existent in the early days of the colonies but were introduced in the eighteenth century. In the private schools, Puritan children were taught reading and writing, religion, Greek and Latin, mathematics, spelling, and proper behavior. Classes were between the hours of eight in the morning and four in the afternoon, with a break for lunch around noon. The classrooms were often without glass windows and were usually dark. Students sat on rough wooden benches and wrote on birch bark since paper was expensive. They used quill pens and ink until pencils were introduced in the nineteenth century. Lessons were recited out loud, and spelling was irregular until Noah Webster wrote his dictionary in the early nineteenth century. A student who gave a wrong answer might be forced to sit in a corner wearing a dunce cap.

One subject taught both at home and in school was manners. Children learned how to walk, eat at the table, and properly address their elders. Books on child raising were written for parents.

Children were brought up on religious books starting with the Bible and followed by John Bunyan's *Pilgrim's Progress.* Another popular religious book was Foxe's *Book of Martyrs*. Well-educated children read Greek, Latin, and the works of great writers such as Alexander Pope, John Milton, and Jonathan Swift. They were expected to go to colleges like Harvard, which was then a divinity school in which young men studied for the min-

In colonial days, the children of the rich did not attend public school but had a private tutor to instruct them.

istry. Good grades were not necessary for admittance. A good family was. Admission was based on class rather than merit. Sons of ministers received first priority followed by sons of magistrates, lawyers, merchants, shopkeepers, seamen, and servants.

Most colonists thought there was no need to educate girls. One father expressed the general feeling when he said, "In the winter it's too far for girls to walk and in the summer, they ought to stay home and help in the kitchen." Another father stated, "The Bible and figgers is all I want my daughter to know." One colonial woman wrote of her childhood, "Female education was conducted on a very limited scale. Girls learned needle point from their mothers and aunts. They are taught to read the Bible and a few are taught to write." Young John Quincy Adams, the future president of the United States, commented that he wished young ladies were as distinguished for the beauty of their minds as well as their personal charm. He compared them to an apple that was beautiful on the outside but "insipid" to the taste.

Corporal punishment was an integral part of a child's education in Puritan America. Teachers had the authority to beat their pupils, and

Until the middle of the nineteenth century, many states did not have public schools. Schoolmasters had great authority over children and could beat them if they thought it necessary.

many did with sadistic delight. They beat children until they vomited or fainted, cracked rulers over children's hands to make them swell so badly that they could not use them for days. Children were beaten with leather straps with a hole in the middle, which caused the flesh to blister. They were beaten with birch rods and sticks, struck on the head and on the soles of their feet. One cruel teacher used to enjoy whipping so much that he would rave as he struck, "Oh, this is good for you!" Another teacher cried out while whipping a student, "This I do to save you from the gallows." As a moral lesson, children were often taken to see adults punished. When a young woman by the name of Betty Smith was arrested for stealing, she was brought to a whipping post in a wheeled cage next door to a school and given thirty lashes on her bare back. The children were brought over to watch and were encouraged by their teachers to throw rotten eggs at the woman.

So powerful was this tradition of physically punishing children that the practice was still in effect long after Puritan rule had ended. In 1829, the clergyman Samuel Arnold published a book called *An Astonishing Affair* in which he attempted to justify the beating of Almon, a four-year-old child he was teaching, for stubbornness.

One day, during a spelling lesson, Almon refused to spell the word *gutter*, a word that he had spelled correctly in the past. The clergyman warned him of the consequences. "You shall obey or I will whip you till you do." But Almon still refused. The clergyman kept his word. "I snapt his ears repeatedly and used various mild measures to obtain obedience." When Almon continued to disobey, the minister took the boy down into the cellar, made him strip, and beat him with birch rods on his bare flesh. "I commenced using the rod according to the Proverb xxiii, 14th, 'Thou shall beat him with the rod and deliver his soul from hell.' I did not think so much of killing him as of saving his life. . . . It was better to break his will than to break my word." Almon refused to yield and the minister then picked up a horsewhip.

> But though the whip was in a bad state, and was so used that it did not break the skin or wound so deeply as the rods, yet my son had no hope that it would wear out. Therefore he submitted and obeyed. He pronounced the words as distinctly and emphatically as I have ever heard from his lips. The relief! The joy! The delightful pleasure it brought! Now I was trans- ported with the thought that he was saved from the jaws of the devourer.

The minister reported that afterward the child was "subdued, . . . unusually mild, submissive, pleasant and interesting. We had a good dinner and he told me, 'I never had anyone so kind to me as you are.'" These may have well been his last words. Two days later Almon died. Unfortunately, the reverend did not record the outcome of his trial. However, many people supported him in his attempt to discipline the child, including Almon's mother.

Despite the prevalence of corporal punishment, northern schools were enlightened when it came to accepting students from a cross sec- tion of the population. In the South, by contrast, education was usually reserved for the children of the wealthy. The children of poor southern whites generally did not go to school. There were a few free schools for children of the poor, which a small number of children attended.

The children of the plantation owners who controlled the South

During slavery, it was forbidden for African-American children to learn to read and write. After emancipation, both children and adults eagerly went to school.

were usually educated by tutors when they were young. Young women were raised to conform to a southern ideal. They were prized for their beauty, modesty, and culture. They did nothing for themselves but depended on their slaves for almost everything. College and a career were out of the question. They were expected to marry young and take care of the household. Girls studied dancing, music, French, sketching, English composition, and literature. A few young women were quite well read and were familiar with the works of great writers like Victor Hugo. Young men were raised to an ideal of southern manhood. They were expected to be excellent horsemen, deadly shots, gallant with the ladies, generous and hospitable, quick tempered, and ready to defend their honor on the dueling field if necessary. Since there were relatively few southern colleges before the Civil War, the sons of wealthy whites went to college either in the North or in England.

Black children in the South, slave or free, were forbidden to attend school. But some managed to secretly educate themselves. When he was nine, Frederick Douglass was sent to Baltimore to serve Hugh Auld, his owner's son-in-law. Auld's wife, Sophia, was a kind and loving woman who, at first, treated him as the child that he was rather than as a slave. When Frederick heard her read the Bible out loud, he asked her to teach him to read. Sophia eagerly responded. She was a deeply religious woman and thought she could teach him to read the Bible. Day by day, Frederick learned the alphabet. He was fulfilling a goal that had been his mother's dream for herself. She had taught herself to read, an accomplishment that Frederick never forgot. "That a field hand had learned to read in a slave state is remarkable—but the achievement of my mother, considering the place and circumstances, was very extraordinary."

Frederick's happiness was not to last. When Sophia Auld told her husband of the great progress Frederick was making, he exploded. He told her that a slave must never learn to read. "Learning will spoil the best nigger in the world. If he learns to read the Bible it will forever unfit him to be a slave. He should know nothing but the will of his master and learn to obey it."

Frederick's brief stay in paradise was over. From that day on, he noticed a change taking place in Sophia.

> The fatal poison of irresponsible power and the radical influence of slave culture were not very long in making their impression on the gentle and loving disposition of my excellent mistress. She regarded me first like a child like any other. Then when she came to consider me as property, our relations to each other were changed.

From being his liberator, Sophia Auld became Frederick's jailer. She spied on his every move to discover if he was reading. If she caught him with a book or a newspaper, she would rip it out of his hands and scold him. The more she tried to prevent him from reading, the more Frederick desired it. He secretly carried a small dictionary with him wherever he went; if he was caught with it, he might be whipped or returned to the plantation. Friendly with a group of neighborhood white children, he recruited them to help him learn. They willingly taught him what they learned at school. Frederick freely discussed with them what he dare not discuss with anyone else—his bitterness at being "a slave for life." He was delighted to discover they agreed with him. "They believed I had as good a right to be free as they had. They did not believe God made anyone to be a slave."

With knowledge came enlightenment but also misery. The more he learned, the more he became aware of the injustice of his condition.

> Light had penetrated the moral dungeon where I had lain and I saw the bloody whip for my back and the iron chain for my feet. . . . The revelation haunted me, stung me and made me gloomy and miserable. It opened my eyes to the horrible pit and revealed the teeth of the frightful dragon that was ready to pounce on me, but alas offered no way of escape. I wished myself a beast, a bird, anything rather than a slave.

Douglass did not remain a slave. As we've seen, he escaped to the North, where he used his education to write about and speak out against the injustices of slavery. He was a great advocate of education for all children.

By the mid-nineteenth century, an education explosion had affected almost all children in the United States, except in the South. Even on the frontier, where the distances were so great that it was difficult for a child to go to school, it was not uncommon for children to ride on horseback or even walk three or more miles to attend class. Children were usually so eager to learn that they willingly traveled the distance. One boy was overjoyed to learn that a teacher had come to his area. "Oh I was so glad. My father told me he wanted me to go every day and I wanted an education so bad. Now I have pulled through this long life in ignorance."

Girls usually outnumbered boys in school because boys were more

For children of the prairies, school was an important part of their lives, even though many had to ride ten or more miles to get there.

likely to stay home and help their fathers in the fields. However, it was not uncommon to see a boy of six sitting next to a man of thirty-four who had decided to learn to read and write despite his age. Most teachers were women. Students learned how to read, spell, and write, and studied geography, grammar, history, Latin, Greek, and mathematics. Communities held spelling bees, which were big events, and the winner received a prize.

In the rougher areas, such as mining towns, older boys often made life difficult for male teachers. They would play practical jokes, such as sawing the legs off a teacher's chair so that when he sat down, the chair would collapse. They wrote insults on the blackboard, made crude jokes in class, and even beat up their teachers on occasion. A teacher who entered the classroom and put a gun on his desk, or one who could whip the strongest boy in class, had a better chance of controlling his students.

Pioneer and frontier children were surprisingly well read. Many of their parents had brought from their original homes books written by famous authors like Charles Dickens, Emile Zola, William Thackeray, and Alexandre Dumas. The two favorites of almost every family were William Shakespeare and the Bible.

Native-American children were taught the traditional ways of their people by their elders, including how to hunt and how to carry out religious ceremonies.

While frontier children often considered their Native-American neighbors as "ignorant," most of the tribes had a very structured system of education for their children. Despite many differences between the two cultures, Native-American children grew up in much the same way as did American children. Girls and boys were raised under a division of labor. Girls learned how to care for the home, cook, make clothes, and craft goods. Boys learned how to hunt and fight. They were taught the religion, history, and traditions in special buildings called lodges. Women were not allowed to enter. In the lodges, the elders told the boys about the origins of their people, how the Great Spirit ruled the earth, and other customs of the tribe. In many tribes, each boy was expected to experience a vision quest. Through fasting and tests of extreme physical hardship bordering on torture, the initiate would hallucinate. In this state, the first animal or natural object that appeared in his fantasy would be his sacred protector. He would adopt a symbol of that animal and wear it into battle.

Like children everywhere, Native Americans were not always enthusiastic about their education. Ah-nen-ladi, a Mohawk boy, grew restless under his grandmother's teaching.

> As I grew older, she took me about in the woods when she went there to gather herbs, and she told me what roots and leaves to collect, and how to dry and prepare them and how to make the extracts and what illness they were good for. But I was tired of such matters and would stray off by myself picking berries and hunting the birds and the little animals with my bow and arrows. So I learned very little from all this lore.

Boys were taught how to hunt game, fight in wars, and live off the land. For some boys, killing their first buffalo was a rite of passage. Luther Standing Bear, whose Lakota Sioux name was Ota K'te (Plenty Kill), was eight years old when his father felt he was ready for the hunt.

> At last the day came when my father allowed me to go on a buffalo hunt with him. What a proud boy I was. I had learned to make bows and arrows and string them. I knew how to ride my pony no matter how fast he would go. I felt I was brave and did not fear danger.

When the men went out, Ota K'te went with them. Suddenly the signal was given for the riders to charge. "Ho-Ka-He!!" Ota K'te raced toward the herd.

> All at once I realized that I was in the midst of buffalo, their dark bodies rushing all about me and their great heads moving

up and down to the sound of their hooves beating upon the earth. Then fear overcame me and I leaned close down on my little pony's body and clutched him tightly. All thoughts of shooting left my mind. In a moment, however, my thoughts became clearer. The buffalo looked too large for me to tackle anyway so I just kept going. My fear was vanishing and I let my pony run. Pretty soon I saw a calf about my size. I was anxious to get it . . . yet afraid to try. I chanced a shot and to my surprise, my arrow landed. My second arrow glanced off the back of the animal. My third arrow hit a spot that made the running beast slow his speed. It seemed to me that I was taking a lot of shots and I was not proud of my marksmanship. I was glad to see the animal going slower and I knew that one more shot would make me a hunter. I was soon by the side of the buffalo . . . and one more shot brought him down.

From the time of colonial days, the elders of many tribes were quick to recognize that the arrival of whites meant the end of the Indians' way of life. Ever since whites first discovered Native Americans, they had been trying to "civilize and Christianize" them, which meant destroying their culture, forcing them to accept that of the Europeans. In the early eighteenth century, the colonists sent Native Americans to Harvard and other colleges to become teachers and instruct their people in the white man's culture. Missionaries went out into the wilderness and built schools. Their goal was to "save the heathen" by converting them to Christianity and forcing them to abandon their own customs. In 1903, Commissioner William Jones made the goal clear.

Give the Indian the white man's chance. Educate him in the rudiments of our language. Teach him to work. Send him to his home and tell him he must practice what he has been taught or starve. It will in a generation or more regenerate the race. It will exterminate the Indian but develop a man.

After the conquest of the tribes by the whites, Native-American children were forced to attend white schools.

Both the government and missionaries attempted to educate many children by isolating them from their tribes, culture, religion, and language. They were sent to boarding schools, often against their will. Some were physically removed from their homes. Many Indian children recalled crying all night long for weeks at the separation. To ensure that the children would attend, Indian police monitored the reservations, and families that did not cooperate were denied the rations and benefits they were entitled to under the treaties, agreements made between Native Americans and the U.S. government.

The world of whites was a culture shock to Native-American children. They encountered a language they did not understand; an institutional world of toilets, baths, sinks, kitchens, and a lack of family. They had to adapt to a new way of dressing, exchanging their moccasins for shoes, wearing pants—which most boys hated—and using buttons (were the buttons to be worn in front or back?). Girls had to have their hair cut. Ztkala-Ka thought short hair disgraceful, worn only by mourners and cowards. She tried to hide but was found under a bed.

> I remember being dragged out, though I resisted by kicking and scratching wildly. In spite of myself, I was carried downstairs and tied fast in a chair. I cried aloud, shaking my head all the time, and heard them gnaw off one of my thick braids. Then I lost my spirit.

The Indian schools were often run like jails and military camps. One student reported:

> There is roll call four times a day. We had to stand at attention or march in step. The B.I.A. [Bureau of Indian Affairs] thought the best way to teach us was to stop us from being Indians. We were forbidden to talk our language or sing our songs.

Teachers were often rigid and harsh disciplinarians. Basil Johnston, an Ojibway, wrote of the isolation, harsh discipline, sadism, and brutality of the priests of his boarding school. He never forgot how his life was regulated by a series of bells, whistles, gongs, and clappers that signaled one activity after another, from the time students got up in the morning until they went to bed at night. The priests' emphasis on authority, discipline, order, and regimentation served one common purpose—to make the students yield and surrender, become subservient and obedient.

Physical punishment was part of the discipline. Some teachers burned children with pokers, beat them until blood flowed, and made them sit with an eraser in their mouth for talking without permission. One student proudly recalled how, despite beatings, he retained his Native-American identity.

> Some teachers hit us on the hands with rulers. A few of these rulers were covered with brass studs. They didn't have much

luck redoing me though. They could make me dress up like a white man but they couldn't change what was inside the shirt and pants. They couldn't make me into an apple—red outside and white inside.

Many Indian children become ill and died at schools. Their immune systems were not able to resist the diseases of the whites. Some ran away and refused to return. A few committed suicide. Others resisted authority whenever and wherever possible. Francis La Flesche remembered the pranks he and other boys played, like deliberately letting the school's pigs loose so that they could take the day off from classes to chase them. The children continued to speak their native language, even though they would be punished if caught. They kept alive the stories and legends of their peoples. Lame Deer refused to accept the Christian religion, insisting on keeping the beliefs of his forefathers. When a priest talked to him about eternity, Lame Deer replied that Indian peoples did not believe in forever and forever. "When my time comes, I want to go where my ancestors are gone." The priest said that may be hell. Lame Deer replied that he would rather be frying with a Sioux grandmother than sitting on a cloud playing a harp with a pale-faced stranger.

As much as they resisted accepting the white man's culture, it was often difficult for Indian children to adjust to their own society after they returned home. Thomas Alford found that his education had alienated him from his family.

There was no happy gathering of family and friends as I so fondly dreamed there would be. Instead of being eager to learn the new ideas I had to teach them, they gave me to understand very plainly they did not approve of me.

Returning children often found that the skills they had learned were not appropriate to life on a reservation. Don Talaveysa, a Navajo, reported:

I . . . discovered that the education had spoiled me for making a living in the desert. I was not hardened to heavy work in the heat and dust and . . . I could not grow young plants in a dry, wind-beaten and worm infested sand drift nor could I shepherd a flock of sheep through storm, drought and disease.

For better and worse, Native Americans were reluctantly forced to give up their own ways and adopt the ways of the whites. But despite doing so, they were often rejected by the white communities whose prejudice against them was profound. Many found themselves in limbo—separated from their traditional ways and rejected by the new society. It is a dilemma that many still struggle with today.

Another group of children who had to struggle with a new culture were the children of immigrants. For those who came to the United States in the late nineteenth century, school was the main road out of the slums and ghettos. It was in schools that immigrant children first learned English. Leonard Covello, who became a famous teacher, found school the means by which he became an American. "I learned arithmetic and penmanship and spelling. . . . I learned how to read in English, learned geography and grammar and all the states in the Union." Covello also learned discipline.

Silence, silence, silence. You never made an unnecessary noise or said an unnecessary word. . . . Lord help you if you broke the rule of silence. I can still see a distant cousin of mine, a girl named Miluzzia, who could never stop talking, standing in a corner through an entire assembly, a spring type clothespin fastened to her lower lip as punishment. Unbowed, defiant Miluzzia with that clothespin dangling from her lip.

Not all children used school as a means to succeed. Harpo Marx, who became an extremely successful actor, decided one day while he was in second grade that he had enough of school. He persuaded two friends to lower him out the window while the teacher stepped out of

Immigrant children learned to become U.S. citizens and speak English by going to school.

the room. He never returned. Harpo found that knowledge he learned in the streets was more important for his survival than what he learned in the classroom.

School didn't teach you what to do when you were stopped by an enemy. It didn't teach you when to run and when to stand your ground. School didn't teach you how to collect tennis balls, build a scooter, ride the trains and trolleys, hitch a ride on the backs of delivery wagons, go for a swim, swipe a chunk of ice or piece of fruit; school didn't teach you what hockshops would give you dough without asking you where you got the goods; school simply didn't teach you to be poor and live from day to day.

In many rural areas, the one-room schoolhouse was the main source of education. A class might have eight grades, and children were divided into small groups according to their age and level of learning.

But for most children, the road out of the slums went through the schoolhouse. As historian David Narsaw pointed out, most children were able to set realistic goals for themselves.

> The children were not fools or dreamers. They did not expect to strike it rich. But neither did they expect to live their lives as their parents lived theirs. They would not be trapped in tenement flats; they would not work all day and then, in the evening, fall asleep exhausted after dinner; they would not allow themselves to be marooned by fear and by debt in slums and ghettoes while the life of the city swirled on around them.

The remarkable thing is that so many made it. They became politicians and actors, business leaders and teachers. Despite the hardships and the pain and misery, they succeeded in life. In part, it was due to their own efforts. In part, it was due to their parents. Leonard Covello, nicknamed Nardo, never forgot his hardworking father's advice. "Nardo. In me you see a dog's life. Go to school. Even if it kills you. With a pen and with books you have the chance to live like a man and not like a beast of burden." Leonard heard his father. He went to school but he also worked, for both were roads to freedom.

I was proud, in Italy was work and work had no hope of a future. A few years of schooling and then work for the rest of your life . . . my case, probably a shoemaker. But here in America, we began to understand that there was a chance, that another world existed beyond the tenements in which we lived and that it was possible to reach out to that world and became a part of it.

If education was the path to success in the immigrant communities it was a path closed to minority children throughout the United States. In the South, there was almost no secondary education for black children, and most elementary schools operated without sufficient funds or teachers. Many southern African-American communities funded their own schools or received partial assistance from foundations. Even in the North, black children attended segregated schools; these were better than those of the South but often inferior to those of white children.

While the philosophy that all children are entitled to an education eventually took hold, it did not apply to children of migrant workers. Most children who labored in the fields did not receive any education. They were on the move too often. Cesar Chavez, who as a child worked the crops with his family, recalled his sporadic schedule.

When we moved to California, we would work after school. Sometimes we wouldn't go. "Following the crops," we missed much school. Trying to get enough money to stay alive the following winter, the whole family picking apricots, walnuts,

Seeing no future for themselves in the job market, many teenagers drop out of school and begin to drift, often becoming involved with drugs.

prunes. . . . We'd go to school two days sometimes, a week, two weeks, three weeks at most. This is when we were migrating. Altogether we had five months out of a total of nine months. We started counting how many schools we had been to and we countered thirty-seven—elementary schools. From first to eighth grade, thirty-seven.

In today's world, getting an education is no longer a problem. Almost every young person is assured of going to school. But the value of that education has come under question. No longer does a high school education guarantee a good job. Now a college education is almost a minimum requirement. In some areas, the schools themselves have become battlegrounds where daily wars are fought between students and teachers, students and students. Where schools once helped unify children of different ethnic backgrounds by Americanizing them, today there is increasing racial and ethnic polarization. African-American, Hispanic, and white parents and educators are fiercely debating whether schools should be racially integrated or separated. The gap between rich and poor schools widens as a large number of students find formal education irrelevant to their lives.

Despite these serious problems, the overall trends in education are encouraging. In the last twenty years there has been a 16 percent increase in the number of students attending college. The dropout rate, once almost 15 percent, has fallen to 11 percent. These statistics, most experts believe, reflect the efforts of teachers and administrators who care about their students and have dedicated themselves to helping them succeed.

8

The Rise and Decline of the Family

I n the Puritan family, the father's word was law. Puritans believed that God made him ruler of his household, answerable to God and no one else—except in extreme cases of abuse or neglect. Children had no rights. John Calvin, the founder of the Puritan faith, made it clear that disobedience to one's parents was a major crime worthy of capital punishment: "Those who violate the parental authority by contempt or rebellion are not men but monsters. Therefore the Lord commands all those who are disobedient to their parents to be put to death."

In Connecticut, a fourteen-year-old child could be hung for disobeying his or her parents. There is no record of the law ever being applied. However, ministers constantly preached that God would visit eternal punishment on a disobedient child. Cotton Mather warned children: "If by Undutifullness to your parents you incur the curse of God, it won't be long before you go down in obscure darkness. God has reserved for you the blackness of Darkness forever."

Parents often quoted the Bible when they punished their children. "Foolishness is in the heart of a child which the rod of correction must early discourage." Puritans believed that because children were born in sin and "natural vessels of depravity," their will had to be broken at an early age in order for them to be saved. One minister advised: "Surely there is in all children a stubbornness arising from a natural pride which must be broken and beaten down that the foundation of their education may in their time be built there."

Yet it would be wrong to conclude that Puritans were unloving parents even if they punished their children severely. Time and again their letters testify to the deep grief they felt at the death of a beloved child, something which almost every Puritan family experienced. One father who lost his three daughters to diphtheria told the congregation in a sermon: "My heart was indeed set upon my children, especially the eldest . . . it pierceth my very heart to call to remembrance the voice of my dear children, calling Father! Father! A voice not now heard."

Many African-Americans were denied the opportunity to establish families because parents and children were often separated and sold to different masters.

The strength of the Puritan family was in its numbers. Because the death rate was so high, the birth rate was even higher. Some families had twenty or more children, although it was extremely rare that all survived.

By the end of the eighteenth century, visitors to this country noted that democracy had a profound effect on family life. The relationships between parents and children were far more easy, and children asserted their independence at an early age. Alexis de Tocqueville, a French visitor to the United States, observed that "in America there is, strictly speaking, no adolescence: at the close of boyhood the man appears and begins to trace out his own path."

De Tocqueville was a great admirer of democracy as he saw it practiced in the United States of the 1840s. He was also keenly aware of what he called an "accursed germ" that existed side by side with democracy—slavery. De Tocqueville warned there were many evils associated with slavery, not the least of which was its impact on African-American family life.

For African-Americans who were enslaved, a normal family life was virtually impossible. A slave family with mother, father, and children was seldom seen. Nehemiah Adams, a New England minister, observed on a trip through the South before the Civil War: "To encourage and protect their homes would be in effect to put an end to slavery as it is. Slaves have no homes!" The slaves' masters deliberately undermined any attempts by blacks to establish family ties. Marriages were not legally recognized by law. Children belonged to the master, not to their parents. Families were broken up and sold on the slave markets. Joseph Henson, who escaped from slavery in 1830 and spent the rest of his life in Canada, remembered the day he and his family were sold at auction after the death of his master.

> My brothers and sisters were bid off one by one, while my mother holding my hand, looked on in an agony of grief. . . . My mother was then separated from me and put up in her turn. She was bought by a man named Isaac R. . . . and then I was offered to the assembled purchasers. My mother, half distracted with the parting forever from all her children, pushed through the crowd while the bidding was going on to the spot where R. was standing. She fell at his feet and clung to his knees, entreating him in tones that only a mother could command, to buy her baby as well as herself and spare to her one of her little ones at least. Can it be believed that this man thus appealed to was capable not merely of turning a deaf ear,

but of disengaging himself from her with such violent kicks and blows, as to reduce her to the necessity of creeping out of his reach and mingling the groan of body suffering with the sob of a breaking heart?

Henson was bought by a stranger and immediately fell so ill that his new master thought he would die. To get back some of the money he had paid for Henson, he sold him cheaply to the man who had bought his mother. Under her care, he recovered.

Frederick Douglass was separated from his mother, who worked as a field hand, shortly after he was born. In his autobiography written years later, entitled *The Life and Times of Frederick Douglass,* Douglass bitterly remarked about his growing up without his real parents.

The process of separating mothers from their children and hiring them out at great distances too great to admit of their meeting, was a marked feature of the cruelty and barbarity of the slave system. It had no interest in recognizing or preserving any of the tie that bind families together. Of my father, I knew nothing. Slavery had no recognition of fathers; the father might be a freeman and the child a slave. The father might be a white man glorifying in the purity of his Anglo-Saxon blood and his child reared with the blackest slaves. He . . . could sell his own child without incurring reproach if in its veins coursed one drop of African blood.

Although black slave families were never officially recognized either by the plantation owner or by the law, there were many illegal marriages. These relationships were seldom respected, and husbands, wives, and children were continually separated from each other. "Slavery provided no means for the honorable repetition of the race," Douglass angrily wrote after he was free.

For white Americans in the nineteenth century, "repetition of the race" was critical. Families continued to be large, and some women gave birth to a child almost every eighteen months for twenty to thirty years. Using the Old Testament as their model, the families were patriarchal and family loyalty was the primary value. For those who journeyed to the unsettled lands of the West, strong families were essential for children to survive the perilous journey.

The pioneer movement across the United States from the 1840s through the 1880s was a family adventure. Sometimes more than a hundred members of an extended family would make the journey together; other times, just parents and their children. They usually traveled in oxen-driven, covered wagons, moving in convoys that could range from as little as twenty-five to as many as one thousand wagons.

The journey was only the beginning of their difficulties. Those that settled in the prairies did not find a paradise with gardens, fruit trees, and running water, but often a flat dry stretch of land that extended from horizon to horizon without a hill, bush or tree to break the monotony. There was no time for disappointment. Families first had to build "sod" houses made out of the earth itself because there were no trees for lumber. They mixed dried earth with grass and roots to make bricks. If they lived near a hill, the family might dig a cave and extend part of it to level ground while the other part was underground. At first, everybody lived in one room. Here the family ate, slept, prayed, worked, made love, and relaxed together.

Living in a sod house was an adventure. Children quickly had to learn how to deal with the hardships of family life. The walls and floors always contained gaps. Snow and rain found their way through the roof; children read by the fire in the winter as snow dropped on their heads or had to wade through several inches of water on the floor after a rainstorm. Other uninvited visitors that came through the cracks included spiders, centipedes, and snakes. Snakes crawled in through the roof and dropped onto the bed. One girl lay down to sleep and found her pillow moving. A nonpoisonous bullsnake had curled up under it. Anne Ellis, who grew up in a mining town, remembered mountain rats dropping between the roof and the canvas that covered the ceiling. Her mother once stuck a fork in the canvas, and Anne saw blood begin to drip through the canvas.

Children were essential to the economic survival of the family. They were needed to carry out important tasks at an early age. By the time children reached five, they were carrying out household chores including cooking, washing, and taking care of

Children were essential to pioneer families, who valued them as laborers as well as for the comfort and joy they provided.

younger children. Hamlin Garland, who became a famous author, wrote in his autobiography, *A Son of the Middle Border*, what it was like for a ten-year-old to plow a field.

> [Plowing] was not a chore but a job. It meant moving to and fro hour after hour, day after day, with no one to talk to but the horses. It meant trudging eight or nine miles in the fore- noon and many more in the afternoon. . . . It meant dragging the heavy implement around corners, and it also meant many shipwrecks. . . . The flies were savage, especially in the middle of the day, and the horses, tortured by their lances . . . often got astride in their traces and made trouble for me.

Gender seemed irrelevant at times. Boys and girls worked in the fields together, planting, harrowing, raking dirt, plowing, pulling weeds, driving birds out of the fields, shucking corn, pitching hay, harvesting and threshing wheat, gathering fuel and wild plants and berries, caring for animals. Boys and girls learned to be very self-reliant at a young age. When Marvin Powers was nine, his father told him to find some runaway horses. Marvin was gone a week, living off the land and camping with some cowboys until he finally returned. When a wolf got caught in her trap, Susie Crockett beat it to death with a tent pole, rather than ask her taunting brothers to do the job. Mary Todd recalled an incident as a teenager involving a dying steer. "I went down to the river. Saw a Texas steer lying on its back alive. It had been there since yesterday so I came up to the house and got the rifle, waded across the river and shot it twice in the head."

Children also made extra money by selling produce and vegetables to nearby towns, gathering buffalo bones for fertilizer, and trading with Indians for furs which they resold. By the time a child was twelve, he or she could carry out most adult responsibilities.

Family life was close. Parents and children lived in a closed universe and drew strength from it. Most families were supportive. In the winter, when there was relatively little work to be done, they gathered around the fire and sang, played games, or read stories to one another. But some parents were also abusive, especially when times were hard and there was a great deal of stress. Crops sometimes failed because of drought or were devoured by plagues of grasshoppers. Cattle froze to death in snowstorms. Children and adults died of disease. Under these and other pressures, men sometimes turned to alcohol. Fathers beat their children. Wives left their husbands, and children ran away and became hoboes, prospectors, or cowboys.

While the pioneer family had to try and preserve itself in the face of natural dangers, immigrant families who flocked from Europe to the United States in the later nineteenth century were faced with the slums of the city with its poverty, violence, alcoholism, and disease.

The struggle of immigrant families to survive was enormous. They lived in unsanitary, overcrowded apartment houses in the slums of the city. Few apartments had their own toilets, and most residents had to

Pioneer life was hard and meager, and a family needed to stay together to survive the harsh climate and environment of the plains.

share a common toilet located either at the end of a hall or in the backyard. Windows in the rear apartments could not be opened because the odor from rotting food—caused by people throwing their garbage out the window into the backyard—was just as bad. But of all the torments, the worst was the vermin. Mike Gold hated bedbugs the most. Despite his mother's heroic efforts to protect him, she could do little.

> One steaming hot night I couldn't sleep for the bedbugs. They have a peculiar nauseating smell of their own; it is the smell of poverty. They crawl slowly and pompously, bloated with blood and the touch and smell of these parasites wakens every nerve to disgust. It was not a lack of cleanliness in the house. The bedbugs were a torment to her. She doused the bed with kerosene, changed the sheets, sprayed the mattress. Nothing could help. The bedbugs lived and bred in the rotten walls of the tenements with the rats, fleas, roaches. They were everywhere.

The strength of the United States throughout its history has been the family. While this family was large, until after the First World War, it was not uncommon for a family to consist of ten to twenty children.

I cannot tell the despair, loathing and rage of the child in the dark tenement room as they crawled on me and stank.

Such conditions put inhuman stress on most families. The pressure broke some families. Many men fell victim to alcoholism and abandoned their families. Many children were abused and neglected, and ran away from home to survive on the city streets. One obstacle that sometimes contributed to alienation between children and their parents was the language barrier. Most children learned English, while many of their parents did not. The experience of Charles Kikuchi, a Japanese child born in the United States, was an extreme example of what happened to many children of immigrants. When Kikuchi's teacher visited his parents' home to discuss their son's lack of progress

/

in his studies because his family did not speak English at home, the father nodded politely a few times, smiling until the teacher left. As soon as she was out the door, he turned on his eight-year-old son with great fury. The teacher's visit had caused him to lose face—the worst thing that could happen to a Japanese—and it was his son's fault. He began to beat the child without mercy.

> As I whimpered, picking myself up after he had kicked me, his rage turned into sadistic passion, and he seized me. I was a disgrace to the race of Nippon! [He said] I was not his son but only my mother's; I had not any Japanese virtue of any sort! In an attempt to remedy this lack, he hung me by the feet to the two by six rafters and whipped me with an old razor strop. I hung there five or ten minutes.

Kikuchi was sent to a Salvation Army semiorphanage. He remained there until he was eighteen. Before he set out on his own, he paid a surprise visit to his parents.

> My mother recognized me at once with a little gasp. She was very still a few seconds, looking at me. Then she closed her eyes and smiled. My father shuffled into the back room from the shop. He did not recognize me. He was only a shadow of the figure he had been ten years before. He was much smaller than I. Like a gnome. When informed who I was, he folded his arms and his head dropped on his sunken chest. I gather he thought that I hated him. Finally, he sat on the edge of one of the brass beds that crowded the room . . . and asked me to forgive him his treatment of me. . . . Then he folded up on the bed and cried.

For those immigrant families that did support each other, a special closeness developed which was never lost. Many parents made great sacrifices for their children, depriving themselves of the basic necessities of life so that their children could go to school and one day make better lives for themselves. Leonard Covello became a teacher because of his parents' support. The Marx brothers never forget the efforts of their mother to help them become comedians. What was surprising was not that so many families disintegrated, but that so many survived and became stronger.

Another group that struggled to survive as a unit was the African-American family. In the 1880s, when slavery had ended and life became more secure for blacks, the percentage of stable two-parent families in the African-American communities roughly equaled that of whites in most cities and rural areas. But over the next twenty years, as the iron grip of segregation was imposed on the black community, and wave after wave of lynchings and riots were unleashed, family life paid the price. Many young men, unable to make a living on the farm, unable to find steady work in the cities, drifted from job to job, became part of the netherworld of crime, or succumbed to alcohol. The pressures of violence and segregation made it difficult at best to maintain a stable family life. It was not until the 1920s, when the country enjoyed a boom period of prosperity, that overt racial violence diminished. But prejudice in the North and South remained intense, and the African-American family still struggled to gain a foothold. One of the ironies was that while black people were excluded from most of the society, their music, both jazz and the blues, helped set the tone for a decade. It was called, appropriately enough, the Jazz Age.

The Jazz Age had a profound effect on family life in urban areas. Young people drank, experimented with sex, danced, and in general pursued the good life, often to the dismay of their parents. The observation that de Tocqueville had made almost eighty years earlier about there being no adolescence in America no longer applied. Middle-class teenagers enjoyed more leisure time than ever before, and much of that was spent away from the family. They identified more with each other than with their elders. Their tastes and attitudes were being shaped by mass media, especially the movies (with their glamorous stars who set the fashions of the day) and radio. The automobile gave them a mobility that young people never had before. The advertising industry recognized teenagers as consumers and appealed to their buying power, giving them a sense of independence. While in many rural areas traditional family values remained, in large towns and cities it seemed as if many parents and their children were headed in different directions.

The Great Depression of the 1930s brought an end to the youth era of the 1920s. The crisis brought many families closer together while driving others farther apart. Rich and middle-class families suffered, as did working-class and poor families. For children of the rich, the greatest shock was usually the loss of their family's fortune. Adele Barker was thirteen when the crash came. She had been raised in luxury in Tennessee with a big house, her own personal servant, and all the toys and clothes she wanted. Suddenly, everything was gone.

> It seemed like everything happened overnight. I had never made a bed in my life. Now I was making my own bed. My mother knew how to cook but she never did the cooking. We had a cook do that. Now my mother was cooking and cleaning. We moved into a smaller house. There was a big quarrel between my parents one night. I didn't know what it was all about. The next day my mother told me we were going to take in boarders.

Enid Wilson grew up the daughter of a rich landowner in the Midwest. She idolized her father, who used to bring her little presents all the time. The presents suddenly stopped. One day she saw her father meeting with strange men behind closed doors. Then everything was gone: the farm, house, money. And then the ultimate tragedy.

> I remember waking up one morning. Everybody was screaming. I got up and looked out the window. Mother was running and my sister was yelling, "Daddy is hanging in the barn."

The worst fear that children had was being separated from their families. Alma Meyer recalled her fear of being sent away.

We children used to be afraid that the family would be broken up and we'd be sent away. We heard of children being sent to live somewhere else because their folks couldn't afford to keep them. So we tried to be extra good so we wouldn't be sent away. I remember I didn't want to make any noise because I was scared that if my parents heard me, they'd know I was there and might send me away, whereas if I was real quiet maybe they would forget about me an I wouldn't have to go. . . . But eventually we were shipped to live with relatives. I told my parents that if they kept me I'd eat only one meal a day so they could save money. I was angry with my dad for sending me away but it wasn't his fault. He tried so hard but the depression was too much. It broke his spirit. It broke my child's heart, I can tell you that.

Despite the hardships, many families became closer. Parents too poor to buy toys made them. If they lacked heat, they would snuggle under the covers in bed. If they couldn't afford to go to the movies, they would read stories to each other. Children were proud to help their families whenever they could. Dale Gene Scales, who as a child migrated from Oklahoma to California and worked in the cotton fields, remembered:

There was no doubt about it. We were poor. We did without. We were hungry a lot of times. But we survived because we stayed close as a family. That made all the difference.

Just as the economy was slowly improving, Americans went to war and children suffered another shock: Their fathers were drafted or enlisted in the armed services. Some husbands and wives had violent arguments when men felt it was their duty to volunteer but their wives

Despite being denied a normal family life for over two hundred years, one of the triumphs of the African-American community has been the building of strong family ties and communities.

thought it was their responsibility to stay home and support their families until they were drafted. Children felt the anguish not only of being separated from their fathers but also of knowing that their fathers could be killed in action.

Ultimately, how children dealt with this separation depended on their mother. Many mothers went to work in war plants, which meant children had to assume a great deal more responsibility for themselves. Teenagers found jobs and helped around the house. For those children whose fathers went to war, their grief was deep and lasted for years. Many were comforted by grandparents who stepped in to fill the absent father's role.

After the war, family life became stable again. At first, there was no generation gap between parents and their children. But in the late 1950s, a national crisis developed when African-American students challenged segregation in the South. They were joined by thousands of young white high school and college students. The conflict with their elders escalated in the 1960s. When fighting began in Vietnam, hundreds of thousands of young Americans defied their parents and protested the war while hundreds of thousands of others were sent overseas to battle. It was the era of the hippie generation. The hippies were young people—many of them students who had dropped out of high school and college—who drifted into the world of sex, drugs, rock and roll. They wore brightly colored clothes, grew long hair, and lived on the streets or in communes. They formed communities that they called "families," which replaced their real families. Many of their parents were deeply upset when their children joined the movement. Some families disowned them; others searched for them, hoping to persuade them to return home. As the war came to an end, the hippie movement gradually died, and by the 1970s, many young people did return to a more conventional life.

But the end of the hippie years did not mean an end to family problems. In the 1980s, the traditional stable family unit was being assaulted by social and economic pressures. The single mother became a national institution as marriages dissolved under financial and emotional pressures. Divorce, which was once regarded with shame, was commonplace. At the same time, teenage pregnancies among the poor increased as young men refused to accept responsibility for the children they helped create. Mothers found themselves responsible for the financial and emotional support of their families. This situation continues to this day and shows no signs of improving. At the present time, 30 percent of all births in the United States are to single mothers. In some cities, over 90 percent of children born to teenage girls will be raised without fathers.

One reason for this trend is the change in community attitudes concerning pregnant single teenage girls. In the 1950s, it was shameful

Some young people who run away from abuse in their homes eventually find their way to shelters like Covenant House where they are helped to get a new start in life.

for a high school girl to become pregnant. She was shunned by "respectable" people and considered an embarrassment to her family. According to a *New York Times* article in 1993, those attitudes have changed radically. "When I was in high school, girls who became pregnant disappeared," said Richard Shuldt, whose teenage daughter, April, was elected homecoming queen in her high school even though she was five months pregnant. "Now my pregnant daughter goes on the Montel Williams show. Today teen pregnancy is being treated like it's no big thing, like it's the norm." One student commented, "There's no reason to mistreat a girl who is pregnant like she has some contagious disease."

Some girls have a baby to establish a close tie. Selma says, "I had my baby because I wanted someone to love who would love me back." Many teenagers resign themselves to living on the welfare program with its guaranteed income, food stamps, health care, and rent supplements. Some are determined to work but often find that the money they earn is not enough for them to even maintain the standard of living they had on welfare.

Many boys show no interest in accepting responsibility for their children though they are proud to have them as a sign of their manhood and a guarantee that their name will be carried on. Imam, a sixteen-year-old involved in the drug trade, commented:

> I want to go out and have me a little son, a little me. Something to be remembered by in case someone come up to me and blow my brains out. I don't know if I'm walking down the street and boom, boom, boom, boom, boom, boom.

While many cities are making a major effort to get young men to accept responsibility for their children, the problem is difficult to solve because many come from broken homes themselves. Having fathers who abandoned them as children, they now abandon their own children. In addition, many do not have steady jobs or are involved in illegal activities. The tragedy is that their children are all the more likely to repeat the same pattern themselves. The close-knit extended family that existed in early times in this country, even the two-parent nuclear family that replaced it in modern times, has no relevance for their lives. The question whether family values as we have traditionally known them can be resurrected is now being debated throughout the United States. In the past twenty-five years, the single-parent family has become more common among most racial groups. White single-parent families have almost doubled from five to almost nine million. Black single-parent families have risen from three to over five million, and Hispanic single-parent families from one million to over two million.

Today, one out of every four women who give birth is unmarried (913,000 out of 3.9 million). Over 80 percent of teenage mothers between fifteen and seventeen and almost 60 percent of eighteen- to nineteen-year-old mothers are not married. Two-thirds of these births are unplanned. Nor is there any sign that the numbers will diminish in the coming years. Religious and community groups, state and federal legislatures are all desperately seeking to end this devastating erosion of traditional family life. It may well be that the future of this nation will depend on whether their efforts are successful.

EPILOGUE

Were children any happier growing up in the past? Yes and no. Many American childhoods have had trouble of one kind or another. Family life might have been better, but health was worse. Schools might have been less violent, but education was poorer. Children were once brutally exploited in the workplace and often at home, and there was little legal protection for them. Racism and prejudice were certainly worse in the past, even though they are still bad today. Patriotism was stronger, but today's teenagers are more critical about the country's military actions. There is now far less restraint and discipline when it comes to sex, but there is also more information available on the subject. Family life in the present is far different from and far worse than the way it was in the past. This problem, perhaps more than any other, can undermine the whole society if left uncorrected. Perhaps, the best that can be said is that American children have made some progress over young people in the past and lost some ground as well. The most significant question, however, is not whether today's children are better off than children in the past, but whether tomorrow's children will be better off than the children of today.

Bibliography

1. Crime and Punishment

Asbury, Herbert. *The Gangs of New York: An Informal History of the Underworld.* New York: Capricorn Books, 1970.

Bing, Leon. *Do or Die.* New York: Harper Perennial, 1991.

Gold, Michael. *Jews Without Money.* New York: Carroll & Graf, 1984.

Wormser, Richard. *Lifers: Learn the Truth at the Expense of Our Sorrow.* New York: Julian Messner, 1990.

———. *Juveniles in Trouble.* New York: Julian Messner, 1992.

2. Dying Young

Bremner, Robert. *Children and Youth in America; a Documentary History.* Cambridge, MA: Harvard University Press, 1970.

Cable, Mary. *The Little Darlings: A History of Child Rearing in America.* New York: Scribners, 1975.

Earle, Alice Morse. *Child Life in Colonial Days,* New York: Macmillan, 1881.

John, Paul Rodman. *A History of Poliomyelitis.* New Haven: Yale, 1971.

West, Elliot. *Growing Up in the Country. Childhood on the Far Western Frontier.* Albuquerque: University of New Mexico Press, 1989.

Wright, Louis. *Everyday Life in Colonial America.* New York: Putnam, 1968.

3. Warrior Children

Bardeen, C. W. *A Little Fifers Diary.* C. W. Bardeen, 1910.

Bishop, Elizabeth. *Ponies, Patriots and Powder Monkeys: A History of Children in the American Armed Forces 1776–1916.* Del Mar, CA: Bishop Press, 1982.

Swann, Brian. *I Tell You Now: Autobiographical Essays by Native American Writers.* Lincoln: University of Nebraska Press, 1987.

Ulmer, George. *Adventures and Reminiscences of a Drummer Boy from Maine.* Chicago: George Ulmer, 1892.

Wormser, Richard. *Three Faces of Vietnam.* New York: Franklin Watts, 1992.

4. SEX AND ROMANCE

Black Elk. *Black Elk Speaks: Being the Life of a Holy Man of the Oglala Sioux.* Lincoln: University of Nebraska Press, 1979.

Bremner, Robert. *Children and Youth in America: a Documentary History.* Cambridge, MA: Harvard University Press, 1970.

Cable, Mary. *The Little Darlings: A History of Child Rearing in America.* New York: Scribners, 1975.

5. WORKING DAYS

Bremner, Robert. *Children and Youth in America: a Documentary History.* Cambridge, MA: Harvard University Press, 1970.

Douglass, Frederick. *Life and Times of Frederick Douglass.* Secaucus, NJ: Citadel, 1983.

Guerin-Gonzales. *Mexican Workers and the American Dream.* New Brunswick, NJ: Rutgers University Press, 1994.

Johnson, Charles. *Shadow of the Plantation.* New York: Schoken, 1941.

Nasaw, David. *Children of the City at Work and at Play.* New York: Doubleday, 1985.

Riis, Jacob. *How the Other Half Lives.* New York, 1900.

Shaw, Nate. *All God's Dangers: The Life of Nate Shaw.* New York: Knopf, 1975.

Terkel, Studs. *Hard Times: An Oral History of the Depression.* New York: Pantheon, 1986.

Wormser, Richard. *Growing Up in the Great Depression.* New York: Atheneum, 1994.

6. HATE THY NEIGHBOR

Gold, Michael. *Jews Without Money.* New York: Carroll & Graf, 1984.

Hopkins, Sarah Winnemucca. *Life Among the Piutes: Their Wrongs and Claims.* Bishop California, Sierra, Media, 1969.

Prewrie, Louise Clark. *Diddie, Dumps and Tot.* New York, 1882.

Ronan, Mary. *Frontier Woman. The Story of Mary Ronan as told to Margaret Ronan.* Missoula: University of Montana Press, 1973.

Sona Monica Itoi. *Nisei Daughter.* Boston: Little Brown, 1953.

Thomas, Dorothy Swain. *Spoilage.* Berkeley: Univ. of California Press, 1946.

———. *Salvage.* Berkeley: Univ. of California Press, 1950.

White, Walter. *A Man Called White.* New York: Arno Press, 1969.

Wright, Richard. *Black Boy.* New York: Harper and Row, 1966.

7. The Struggle to Learn

Arnold, Samuel. *An Astonishing Affair*. Concord, NH, 1830.

Bremner, Robert. *Children and Youth in America; a Documentary History*. Cambridge, MA: Harvard University Press, 1970.

Covello, Leonard. *The Heart Is the Teacher.* New York: McGraw Hill, 1958.

Douglass, Frederick. *Life and Times of Frederick Douglass*. Secaucus, NJ: Citadel, 1983.

Le Flesche, Francis. *The Middle Five: Indian Schoolboys of the Omaha Tribe*. Madison: University of Wisconsin Press, 1900.

Marx, Harpo. *Harpo Speaks*. London: Gollancz, 1967.

Standing Bear, Luther. *My Indian Boyhood*. Lincoln: University of Nebraska Press, 1988.

8. The Rise and Decline of the Family

Bremner, Robert. *Children and Youth in America: a Documentary History*. Cambridge, MA: Harvard University Press, 1970.

Douglass, Frederick. *Life and Times of Frederick Douglass*. Secaucus, NJ: Citadel, 1983.

Garland, Hamlin. *Son of a Middle Border*. New York: Penguin, 1995.

Tuttle, William. *Daddy's Gone to War: The Second World War in the Lives of American Children*. New York: Oxford University Press, 1993.

Warner, Luna. *The Diary of Luna Warner, A Kansas Teenager of the Early 1870s*. Kansas Historical Society (Autumn and Winter, 1969).

West, Elliot. *Children and Adolescents in America, 1850–1950*. Lawrence: University of Kansas Press, 1992.

Wormser, Richard. *Growing Up in the Great Depression*. New York: Atheneum, 1994.

INDEX